ON AWARENESS

ON AWARENESS

A Collection of Philosophical Dialogues

Nicholas J. Pappas

Algora Publishing
New York

Library of Congress Cataloging-in-Publication Data —

Pappas, Nicholas J.
   On awareness: a collection of philosophical dialogues / Nicholas J. Pappas.
      p. cm.
      ISBN 978-0-87586-840-0 (soft: alk. paper) — ISBN 978-0-87586-841-7 (hard: alk.
paper) — ISBN 978-0-87586-842-4 (ebook) 1. Philosophy—Miscellanea. 2. Awareness—
Miscellanea. 3. Belief and doubt—Miscellanea. 4. Integrity—Miscellanea. I. Title.
   B68.P35 2011
   100—dc22
                         2010050438

Front cover: © Michael Kloth/Corbis

Printed in the United States

To the memory of my father, James Zisi Pappas

TABLE OF CONTENTS

INTRODUCTION

This is a book of thirty-one short philosophical dialogues, marking a departure for me. My previous two books with Algora contained dialogues of much greater length. Why the change?

Many people today lead busy lives. Accordingly, it's nice to be able to read five pages or so and reach an end. The book may then be set down and picked up another time. Or, one might carry on with another morsel, depending on time available and how one feels.

From my perspective, the shortness of the dialogues afforded me the opportunity to explore many themes. A glance through the table of contents of this book gives an idea of what these themes are. But is there a larger theme?

Awareness. Most of the dialogues in this book deal with being aware of, or knowing, many things — things that might be all too obvious, or things that might not be obvious at all. Consider the dialogue called Knowing. Is it harder to know than not to know? What do you do with experiences that are difficult to come to terms with? Do we have a choice concerning our awareness of such experiences?

While the dialogues may suggest answers to questions such as these, they do not profess to be authoritative. Director, the one constant character throughout the dialogues, perhaps comes closest to being an authority on the themes explored. And yet his dialogue depends on the opinions of

Friend and the other interlocutors.

A note on Friend. He is not necessarily the same Friend in each dialogue. Director has many Friends.

I hope you enjoy the book.

Nick Pappas

WAIT

Persons of the Dialogue

Director

Friend

1

Friend: When do you have to wait?

Director: When things aren't ready.

Friend: What things?

Director: The things in question.

Friend: Yes, but what things are in question?

Director: The things concerning people.

Friend: You mean the people themselves.

Director: Yes, the people themselves.

Friend: What of people has to be ready?

Director: Their knowledge.

Friend: Their knowledge of what?

Director: Themselves.

Friend: So you don't want anything to do with people who don't have knowledge of themselves?

Director: I prefer people who have knowledge of themselves.

Friend: And yet you spend time with people who don't have knowledge of themselves.

Director: True.

Friend: Why?

2

Director: I hope to help them arrive at knowledge of themselves.

Friend: How do you do this?

Director: I challenge their false views.

Friend: And that's enough?

Director: It's enough, with some, to sow the seed of doubt.

Friend: What need do they have for doubt?

Director: They think they know themselves but they don't.

Friend: How do you know?

Director: I know people.

Friend: So when you get these people to doubt what they think they are, they arrive at knowledge of what they really are?

Director: In the best case, yes.

Friend: They don't all succeed?

Director: No.

Friend: Why not?

Director: Because some people are in love with what they think they are.

Friend: Falling out of love is no easy thing.

Director: No, it's not.

3

Friend: Do the people who fall out of love with their image of themselves resent you?

Director: I don't know.

Friend: Why not?

Director: Because I'm not around when this happens.

Friend: What, do you make yourself scarce?

Director: No, the person in question usually goes off on his own, alone.

Friend: In order to work things out.

Director: Yes.

Friend: Does he then return if he is successful?

Director: Often times, yes.

Friend: What then? You are friends?

Director: We are friends.

Friend: What if the person in question is unsuccessful?

Director: I keep waiting.

Friend: How long do you wait?

Director: In some cases, many years.

Friend: Is the waiting difficult?

Director: I find ways to divert myself.

4

Friend: What does it mean to work things out?

Director: It means letting go of the old image of oneself and embracing the new.

Friend: Like a butterfly emerging from a cocoon?

Director: Something like that.

Friend: This is difficult psychological work?

Director: Very.

Friend: And that is why you are patient and wait.

Director: Yes.

Friend: What makes you impatient?

Director: People who come back to me before they have finished their work.

Friend: Why does that make you impatient?

Director: Because they know deep down inside that they haven't finished their work, and are looking for a shortcut.

Friend: And no shortcuts exist.

Director: Actually, shortcuts do exist. That's what makes it harder.

Friend: Harder to stay on track to complete the work?

Director: Yes.

5

Friend: So your waiting is over when they complete their work.

Director: It is.

Friend: And what do you have then?

Director: I have a friend, a true friend.

Friend: But you were friends before, no?

Director: We were. But now we are better, truer friends.

Friend: Because you both have knowledge of yourselves.

Director: Yes.

Friend: Do you spend lots of time together now that your waiting is done?

Director: No, actually only a little amount of time.

Friend: Why?

Director: Because now my friend has more work to do.

Friend: What work?

Director: Going off and doing for others what I did for him.

Friend: What exactly did you do for him, again?

Director: I told him the truth.

Friend: About himself?

Director: Yes.

6

Friend: Tell me more about this truth.

Director: Suppose he thinks he is terribly handsome, but he's not. I tell him he's not. And so on.

Friend: What if he thinks he is plain when in fact he is terribly handsome? Do you bolster his ego?

Director: I just tell him the truth, whatever it may be.

Friend: Do you tell him the truth about the quality of his mind? I mean, suppose he thinks he is the smartest man in the world.

Director: I tell him there are others with mental qualities like his.

Friend: Even if he is the smartest man in the world?

Director: I don't believe there is a single smartest person in the world. I make that clear to him.

Friend: Have you ever really talked to someone who thought he was the smartest person in the world?

Director: I have.

Friend: What could possess someone to think that?

Director: Isolation.

Friend: What, was he a hermit?

Director: No, he just built up a wall inside his mind.

7

Friend: And you told him he needed to take it down.

Director: Yes — stone by stone.

Friend: And they are heavy stones?

Director: His were very heavy, yes.

Friend: So what does it take for someone to take a wall like that down?

Director: Patience.

Friend: Why?

Director: Each time you take a stone down, because of the great exertion required, you have to rest sufficiently before you attempt to take down the next.

Friend: Did the wall reach all the way around his mind?

Director: Almost. I met him when the last section was about to be finished.

Friend: So you got through to him just in time.

Director: Yes.

Friend: What did you do, stand at the gap and call in to him?

Director: No, I just walked right in.

Friend: Really? Wasn't that rather shocking to your friend?

Director: He stood in need of a shock.

Friend: What does the "just walked right in" metaphor stand for?

8

Director: I got inside his head, as they say.

Friend: Yes, but how?

Director: I listened closely to what he was saying. Then I showed him I understood what he was talking about, where he was coming from.

Friend: I take it that no one had done that before with him.

Director: That's right. I was the first to really get through to him.

Friend: And then you told him to be patient and take down that wall.

Director: Yes.

Friend: Was he afraid of being without his defense?

Director: Yes, but I started to teach him that offense is the best defense.

Friend: Started to teach him?

Director: He went off on his own after the first lesson.

Friend: Do you think that one lesson was enough?

Director: I think so.

Friend: Of what does this offense consist?

Director: Most of the time it consists of a great deal of waiting.

Friend: Waiting for what?

Director: Opportunity to challenge false views.

Friend: Aren't there plenty of false views to choose from at any given moment?

Director: There are. But not all people are open to being challenged all the time.

Friend: So you wait for an opening.

Director: Yes. I wait.

EXPAND

Persons of the Dialogue

Director

Student

1

Student: When should you expand on what you've said?

Director: Usually when clarity requires you to do so.

Student: So if I've been perfectly clear, and someone asks me to expand, I should refuse?

Director: It's generally considered a friendly gesture to expand under those circumstances.

Student: What if I'm not talking to a friend?

Director: Then you can simply repeat what you've already said or say nothing. That's what an oracle would do.

Student: You think I should act like an oracle?

Director: I'm just saying — that's what an oracle would do.

Student: So you're refusing to expand on what you've said?

Director: Yes.

Student: But we're friends. Why won't you expand?

Director: I thought I was sufficiently clear.

Student: Yes, but I don't get the point of what you said.

Director: Then you'll have to think about it some more.

2

Student: Here's what I think. You don't want me to act like an oracle. The point is that you should always expand when requested to do so.

Director: Why?

Student: Because the person making the request might really want to understand you, and you're obliged to help him if you can.

Director: But you wanted to understand my oracle comment. And I said nothing further about it.

Student: Are you saying the point isn't what I think it is?

Director: I will neither confirm nor deny.

Student: So you're going to continue to play the oracle.

Director: Yes.

Student: Why do you want to do this?

Director: Because I want you to come to your own conclusion.

Student: But I have.

Director: You really want me, as a friend, to expand for you?

Student: Yes.

Director: Very well, then. As a friend I will say more. You seem to think you are obliged to help everyone understand by expanding on what you've said. I don't think you are.

3

Student: You think it's perfectly up to you whether you expand or not.

Director: Yes.

Student: And you generally will only expand for friends.

Director: Generally, yes.

Student: When do you make exceptions?

Director: Whenever I think someone really and truly wants to know — in other words, deserves to know.

Student: And not everyone deserves to know. But how can you tell which is which?

Director: There are signs.

Student: What signs?

Director: The deserving engage in earnest questioning and an independent effort to understand.

Student: What happens if you expand as much as possible for someone like that, and he still doesn't understand?

Director: We keep trying. For important things, at least, you never really run out of ways to expand.

Student: Suppose the person you're talking to comes to understand. Does he then go around expanding on this for everyone he meets, out of enthusiasm?

Director: That sometimes happens.

4

Student: What are the consequences of expanding to people who don't deserve to know?

Director: There might be backlash.

Student: What sort of knowledge are we talking about that there might be backlash?

Director: Knowledge about human nature and how it manifests itself in our world.

Student: People who don't really want to know about this don't want to know for a reason.

Director: That's right.

Student: And that reason, basically, is that they are bad human beings?

Director: In my opinion, anyway.

Student: It's ironic. They don't really want to know, but they want us to expand.

Director: They many times want to catch us up in our own words, as in a net.

Student: Are these the people for whom you refuse to expand?

Director: Often times, yes.

Student: When else do you refuse to expand?

Director: I refused to expand for you. Why?

Student: You were trying to teach me a lesson.

Director: Do you agree that that's a good reason not to expand?

5

Student: I'm not sure. What harm would have come from expanding for me?

Director: Probably not much, if any. But you might not have revealed what you were thinking.

Student: You wanted to flush out my erroneous opinion.

Director: Yes.

Student: But you could have just asked me what I think.

Director: I don't think that would have had quite the same effect.

Student: You mean you wouldn't have had quite the same fun.

Director: Well, there's some truth to that.

Student: Do you think it's alright to have fun at your friend's expense?

Director: At your expense? Really, Student, were you wounded by what I said?

Student: No.

Director And our conversation moved forward productively?

Student: Yes.

Director: And now you realize that you don't have a duty to expand for just anyone?

Student: Yes, but I'd like to understand more fully why.

Director: Think of it this way. Some things are meant for you and your good friends only. Would you share what is most precious to you with an indifferent or even hostile stranger?

6

Student: No, I wouldn't. But what is most precious to me?

Director: You mean you don't know?

Student: I want to hear what you think. I want you to expand on what you are saying.

Director: Alright, Student. If a hostile stranger asks you what is most important to you, you might well answer that it is your friends. But then he asks you to expand on that. He asks you to name your friends and where they live. Would you?

Student: Certainly not.

Director: Imagine that scenario as a metaphoric template for other things you might be asked to expand on. Can you do that?

Student: Yes, and I think I know exactly what you mean. You can give a hostile stranger general information but must hold back on the specifics.

Director: And why do we hold back on the specifics?

Student: Because he hasn't earned the right to know them.

Director: Why else?

Student: We're concerned for safety.

Director: Friends look out for one another.

Student: They do.

Director: Might that be a reason why a friend doesn't expand with a friend?

Student: What do you mean?

7

Director: I mean, you might not expand with a friend out of concern for his safety.

Student: You mean you wouldn't give him information that would endanger him?

Director: Yes.

Student: What kind of information have you got in mind?

Director: Suppose a friend is worked up into a frenzy of anger and wants to start a fight with a powerful enemy. He asks me if I know good methods of attack. I tell him I do. He then asks me to expand, to show him these methods. I refuse.

Student: I see what you mean.

Director: So we have a reason why one might not expand.

Student: We do.

Director: But still, the general rule is to expand with friends, and say nothing more than the minimum to enemies — no expanding.

Student: And so we'd better pick our words to enemies carefully.

Director: More carefully than to friends?

Student: When you intend to say nothing more, that's when you have to be most careful.

8

Director: But even when you intend to expand, don't you have to be careful, too? Aren't words once said hard to take back?

Student: Yes, that's true.

Director: So we always speak with care.

Student: We always try to speak with care.

Director: What stops us from speaking with care?

Student: Another sort of expansion — an expansive mood.

Director: Expansive moods make us expand on what we say indiscriminately?

Student: Sometimes they do. We must guard against that.

Director: Even among friends?

Student: Even among friends, but especially among others.

Director: But aren't we typically more expansive among our friends?

Student: We are.

Director: So we have to take equal care among friends and enemies alike?

Student: I think that's best.

OPEN

Persons of the Dialogue

Director

Heir

1

Director: What does it mean to be open?

Heir: It means you share what you are thinking.

Director: Is it always good share what you are thinking?

Heir: No.

Director: When is it good to share, to be open?

Heir: When you're among friends.

Director: And it's bad to be open among enemies?

Heir: Yes.

Director: What about among neutrals?

Heir: You can share selectively.

Director: How do you know what to select?

Heir: You have to exercise your judgment.

Director: What is your judgment based upon?

Heir: What is typically deemed acceptable.

Director: So you just exchange fashionable opinions with neutrals?

Heir: More or less.

2

Director: But wouldn't you like to win some of these neutrals over as friends?

Heir: Sure. How?

Director: Venture some of your private opinions. Be more open with them.

Heir: What if they have a negative reaction?

Director: Then you can always back off and stick with fashionable opinions. But what if they have a positive reaction? They might open up a bit, too, and share some of their private opinions. Isn't that what makes for friendship, openness?

Heir: Yes, among other things.

Director: What other things?

Heir: Loyalty.

Director: So if you open up with an opinion about a controversial topic, one your friends don't care for, they will remain your friends out of loyalty?

Heir: That's the idea.

Director: Is loyalty something you think or something you feel?

Heir: I suppose it's something you feel.

Director: Isn't part of opening up sharing what you feel? In other words, it's not just about what you think.

Heir: Yes, it's also about what you feel.

Director: Are thought and feeling the only two aspects of openness?

Heir: Yes, I think they are.

3

Director: Now, when you meet a stranger, do you attempt to be open with him or do you simply stay closed no matter what he says or does?

Heir: If he shows signs of openness I would attempt to be open with him to some degree.

Director: What do you open up about first, thoughts or feelings?

Heir: I would start with the safer of the two, thoughts.

Director: Why are thoughts safer than feelings?

Heir: Because feelings can be volatile.

Director: But aren't certain thoughts attached to certain feelings?

Heir: They can be, but I try not to have the two connect like that.

Director: You mean your thoughts are separate from your feelings?

Heir: Yes.

Director: Tell me something you think.

Heir: I think our current leader is no good.

Director: If some people disagree with you about that, would it upset you?

Heir: No. My thoughts and feelings are separate.

Director: What if some people got upset with you for stating that opinion about the leader? Would that upset you?

Heir: Probably.

4

Director: Then would you say that your thoughts and feelings are connected, but at a remove?

Heir: No. My getting upset has nothing to do with my thought. It has to do with their getting upset.

Director: Yes, but it was your thought that got them upset in the first place.

Heir: That doesn't change the fact that my thoughts are separate from my feelings.

Director: How do you know the difference between thoughts and feelings?

Heir: What do you mean?

Director: Suppose someone comes up to you and says that the current leader is good. How would you know if that represents a thought or a feeling?

Heir: I would have to probe. If it's a feeling, there's nothing else behind it. If it's a thought, there are reasons backing it.

Director: What if those reasons are, in turn, backed by feelings?

Heir: If they are, then the reasons are not of as high a quality as they would be if they were backed by reasons.

Director: So you have to have reasons for the reasons.

Heir: Yes.

Director: And you need reasons for the reasons for the reasons.

Heir: Yes, you keep on going until you have gotten rid of all the feeling.

Director: This is what you have done.

Heir: I have. Nothing but reason remains.

Director: In one half of your mind.

Heir: True.

Director: Does your reason feel pressure from the other half where your emotions are?

Heir: Some, but doesn't everyone?

Director: No. Not everyone has created this divide between reason and emotion.

Heir: You're a philosopher. Haven't you?

5

Director: I don't think I've created a divide like you have, Heir.

Heir: I thought keeping reason and emotion separate was one of the prime objectives of philosophy.

Director: In my view, philosophy involves them both.

Heir: Interesting. I'll have to think about this. But let's get back to what we were talking about, something that has been bothering me.

Director: What?

Heir: Suppose I'm open with someone, but he is not open with me.

Director: You mean, for instance, what if he is upset with what you are saying but hides how he feels?

Heir: Yes.

Director: You can ask him how he feels if you suspect this. He may follow your lead and tell you simply.

Heir: But what if he doesn't tell me the truth about what he feels?

Director: You mean, what if he pretends to be open with you?

Heir: Yes.

Director: Well, then you must be prepared to be fooled.

Heir: What?

Director: Yes, you must allow yourself to be fooled.

Heir: But why?

6

Director: What are the consequences the other way?

Heir: You mean of being suspicious, of being afraid?

Director: Yes.

Heir: I suppose the suspicion and fear can get out of control.

Director: Yes, and quickly, too, depending on who you're talking to.

Heir: So you want me to take people at face value, take them at what they say.

Director: Yes. That's part of being open, too, isn't it?

Heir: I suppose. But I have to tell you, Director, I don't like it.

Director: What's the worst that can happen?

Heir: Someone with other thoughts and sentiments can infiltrate my circle of friends.

Director: Infiltrate is a very serious sounding word.

Heir: It's a serious problem.

Director: Why? Suppose someone not truly of your views has dinner with you and your friends. Assuming we're not talking about a criminal or a terrorist, what's the harm? Besides, how long do you think someone like that can keep up his act?

Heir: Oh, I think he can keep it up a good long while. Some people don't even know what they really think or feel, so they dress themselves up in the thoughts and feelings of others to cover their nakedness.

Director: Don't you feel sorry for them?

Heir: You can feel sorry for them and not want anything to do with them at the same time.

7

Director: So what does this mean? You'll never venture out of your circle of friends to see if there are others out there you might like to spend time with?

Heir: No, I'm not saying that.

Director: Suppose you don't allow yourself to be fooled by what someone else says. What does that involve?

Heir: You try to catch him up in what he says, to see if he is lying to you.

Director: So you're not being an open listener. You're something of a partially closed listener.

Heir: Yes.

Director: Are you a fully open listener when you are among your own, within your own circle of friends?

Heir: I am, for the most part.

Director: And what about speaking? Are you fully open about your thoughts and feelings?

Heir: Again, for the most part.

Director: What holds you back?

Heir: Nothing is perfect, Director.

Director: It is the rare friend with whom you can be fully open, both listening and speaking?

Heir: It is, if such a friend is in fact not merely a dream.

PEACE

Persons of the Dialogue

Director

Friend

1

Director: When are you at peace?

Friend: When there is nothing I have done, or haven't done, that bothers me.

Director: If something bothers you, how do you make it stop?

Friend: I correct the situation.

Director: What if you can't?

Friend: Then I have to learn to live with my mistake.

Director: What if you do something that isn't a mistake, that's right, and it still bothers you?

Friend: Why would it do that?

Director: Because you might be in the habit of doing this particular thing the wrong way. Doing it the right way goes against your grain.

Friend: I see. Well, in that case, I would have to find a way to persuade myself to fully accept that it's the right thing.

Director: Is that something like learning to live with a mistake?

Friend: Oddly, yes — but it's also the opposite of that.

Director: How do you know something you are used to doing is wrong?

Friend: Someone might convince me it is.

Director: Someone you trust.

Friend: Yes, someone like you.

2

Director: Now, it may feel wrong, as we've said, when you try to correct a wrong.

Friend: Yes.

Director: So you might not be at peace until the new way becomes a habit, until the new way feels right.

Friend: That's right.

Director: How long do you think it takes to get comfortable with a new way?

Friend: I think that depends on what it involves. It could be days, weeks, months, or years.

Director: Would it have to be something serious to take years?

Friend: Probably.

Director: What if you have more than one thing that's wrong?

Friend: I would try to correct them one at a time, so I don't become overwhelmed.

Director: How would you pick what to start with?

Friend: It might be best to start with something relatively easy and work my way up to the harder things.

Director: But wouldn't it weigh on you to know that the hard ones were waiting? Wouldn't the hard ones likely affect your peace the most?

Friend: That's a good point. Maybe it's best to start with the hardest.

Director: Yes. But, then again, to get at the hardest one, maybe it's necessary to get some of the easiest ones under control first.

Friend: What do you mean?

3

Director: What if you have many relatively easy to deal with disturbances, things that are like mosquitoes? Might there not come a point when you have so many mosquitoes, disturbing your peace such, that you can't get to your hardest issue?

Friend: In that case I'd have to put up a net to stop them.

Director: What does this net stand for in real life?

Friend: I'm not sure.

Director: What does a net create?

Friend: An enclosed area.

Director: If you are in an enclosed area, what happens?

Friend: Your contacts with those outside are limited.

Director: They are limited to those you let in?

Friend: Yes.

Director: What if you let someone in and a mosquito comes along with him?

Friend: Then first order of business, for both of us, is to kill the mosquito.

Director: What if many mosquitoes come in?

Friend: It makes no difference. The first thing we have to do is kill the mosquitoes.

Director: What if the person you let in believes it is wrong to kill mosquitoes?

Friend: I would ask him to leave.

4

Director: You'll only invite in people who are willing to kill the mosquitoes they may have brought in with them.

Friend: Yes.

Director: Whose peace do the mosquitoes disturb?

Friend: Everyone's in the enclosure.

Director: One person's not being at peace can affect another's peace.

Friend: Yes.

Director: So, not only do we have an obligation to ourselves to be at peace, we have an obligation to others, too?

Friend: It's funny, but I've never thought about it that way. I think that's absolutely true. We all need to be at peace. But isn't that just a dream?

Director: Perhaps. But what would it take to make steps in that direction?

Friend: Honesty.

Director: Can you say more?

Friend: People need to be honest with themselves and others about whether they are at peace, and if not, what the source of trouble is.

Director: Because if others know the source they might be able to help?

Friend: Yes.

5

Director: And others would be willing to help because it would improve their own sense of peace.

Friend: Exactly.

Director: This would take a healthy amount of trust, wouldn't it?

Friend: Very much so.

Director: What are the grounds for this trust?

Friend: Well, you would likely open up about your lack of peace only to friends.

Director: Because you already trust them.

Friend: Yes.

Director: And there are professionals, are there not, who we are supposed to trust to help us with our peace?

Friend: There are. But I would trust my friends over them.

Director: Why?

Friend: Because I know them better.

Director: What if you get to know one of these professionals?

Friend: How can you? It's a one way street when you talk to them. You only talk about you. They never talk about themselves.

Director: So you only know them insofar as they talk about you.

Friend: Yes, and that's not enough for me to trust.

6

Director: But can't you say things to them that you can't say to your friends?

Friend: If that's the case, then I haven't got the right friends.

Director: The right friends are hard to come by, no?

Friend: Very hard to come by.

Director: Maybe that's why these professionals are needed. Not everyone has the right friends.

Friend: That's a good point.

Director: Now, we're saying that everyone has a duty to help themselves, and that everyone has a duty to help others?

Friend: Yes, but only the others we let in to our space, our enclosure.

Director: How do you know if you can help someone with his peace?

Friend: I think all you can do is try. Sometimes you'll help. Sometimes you won't.

Director: And when you don't help, is there a risk you'll make matters worse?

Friend: There is.

Director: So you have to be careful.

Friend: I agree.

Director: What does this care consist of?

Friend: Not giving advice until you really know what the problem is.

7

Director: So you have to be willing to watch a person suffer from lack of peace until you're sure what the problem is?

Friend: Yes, and it's no fun for you while watching.

Director: What makes you sure about the problem? Couldn't you be wrong?

Friend: Yes, of course you could.

Director: Is there any way to be sure?

Friend: You can try your hunch out.

Director: Would you go in hot and heavy with whatever you might recommend?

Friend: No, no. You go in with a light touch, just to feel things out a little. If you're wrong, a light touch will be enough to let you know it. A person suffering from lack of peace is very sensitive, after all. If you're right, though, you'll also know it. Then you can open up more fully, if the gentle touch wasn't enough.

Director: Is it a good example of a light touch if I say, "I don't think you're good at creating and maintaining necessary personal boundaries, and it's affecting your peace."

Friend: I think that might be fine, depending on the circumstances.

Director: What if the circumstances are these circumstances, this here and now?

Friend: You're saying this to me?

Director: I'm saying this to you.

Friend: Wow! You caught me off guard. But I think there's truth in what you say. Can you say more?

DREAD

Persons of the Dialogue

Director

Friend

1

Director: What is dread?

Friend: Fear in anticipation of something.

Director: In anticipation of what?

Friend: Anything that causes fear.

Director: What causes fear?

Friend: Having to face something.

Director: Having to face what?

Friend: You're not going to let me off easy here, are you? Having to face something that you think will be unpleasant.

Director: You're afraid of the unpleasant?

Friend: That's the thing about dread. Things seem worse in anticipation than they often turn out to be.

Director: Why do you think that is?

Friend: Because your imagination runs wild. You think of all the things that can go wrong.

Director: And usually only some, if any, of those things go wrong?

Friend: Yes.

Director: If you get your imagination under control, will you get your dread under control, too?

Friend: I suppose you will.

2

Director: How do you get your imagination under control?

Friend: You can't let it become one sided. I mean, for every bad thing you imagine, you should make a point of imagining one good thing, too.

Director: So the net effect is to cancel imagination out, good balancing bad.

Friend: Yes. It's just that many people have a hard time imagining the good.

Director: Why do you think that is?

Friend: Because fear is often times stronger than hope.

Director: But for some people hope is stronger than fear.

Friend: Yes.

Director: What makes someone incline to one or the other?

Friend: I would say it's a combination of natural temperament coupled to habit.

Director: Can you change your natural temperament?

Friend: No.

Director: But you can certainly change your habits.

Friend: Certainly, though not easily.

3

Director: So how do we get those who dread to start hoping?

Friend: I think they have to work to see positive possibilities.

Director: So if someone dreads going to work, all he has to do is start seeing positive possibilities in the office, and he will start to lose his dread?

Friend: It's not quite that simple. As he sees the positive he will start doing positive things, and these positive things will bring about positive results, leading him to dread less.

Director: What if he sees lots of positive things, and starts doing positive things, but gets no positive results?

Friend: Assuming he gives it long enough, then I would say he is in the wrong job.

Director: You're in the right place when your positive efforts bring about positive results.

Friend: Yes.

Director: And positive results fight dread.

Friend: They certainly do.

Director: What if your idea of positive results differs from the dominant idea of positive results in the place in which you find yourself?

Friend: What do you mean?

Director: Suppose you are a manager of a team. Your idea of positive results is if everyone on your team is relatively happy and thriving in his role. But the company only cares about numbers, and the more your team thrives the more the company squeezes, to the point where the team is no longer happy or thriving any more. Might you not start to dread coming to work?

Friend: I think you might.

4

Director: So you're in the wrong place if your positive results aren't appreciated.

Friend: You are.

Director: What else might you dread about work?

Friend: People trying to undermine you.

Director: That's understandable. What else?

Friend: Having to make a presentation.

Director: Why would you dread that?

Friend: Because you're afraid you're going to mess up.

Director: Let's consider these last two examples — people trying to undermine you, and making a presentation. They are two very different things.

Friend: Yes, but they produce the same result.

Director: I can understand how you would imagine you are going to mess up on your presentation. But tell me about how you might imagine people are undermining you. Are you saying you're paranoid?

Friend: Oh, no. I'm talking about a situation where you know, where you have proof, that people are trying to undermine you.

Director: And you find facing them unpleasant.

Friend: To put it mildly, yes. You dread facing them.

Director: But you didn't do anything wrong?

Friend: That's right.

5

Director: Can't you let the rightness of your cause triumph over the dread?

Friend: Rightness is one thing. Hope is another.

Director: Ah, you have no hope that their behavior will change. So what will you do, leave?

Friend: That may be the only option.

Director: We've talked about being in the wrong place a few times now. And when it's clear you're in the wrong place, you need to go. Right?

Friend: Right.

Director: But what if, for whatever reason, you can't leave?

Friend: You're going to have to find a way to overcome your dread.

Director: Is hope the best means?

Friend: It's the best I can think of right now.

Director: So how do we get hope in a hopeless situation?

Friend: I think we first have to come to terms with how bad the situation really is.

Director: Because false hope will do us no good?

Friend: Exactly. Once you make it clear to yourself that there are no grounds for hope, you then, ironically, start looking for hope.

Director: And where will you find it?

Friend: In simple things, basic interactions with people. You keep your feet planted firmly on the ground.

6

Director: If you've never really had your feet planted on the ground, wouldn't a sort of hope come from doing this for the first time?

Friend: Yes, I think it would.

Director: Do you think many people have their feet planted firmly on the ground?

Friend: No, in my experience, not many.

Director: Is that because they are carried away by hopes?

Friend: Some of them are, yes.

Director: What about the rest?

Friend: They are the ones who dread.

Director: Why aren't their feet on the ground?

Friend: Because the dread has them lying down flat on their backs.

Director: So the overly hopeful need to get their feet down on the ground from up in the air. And the ones who dread need to stand up and walk.

Friend: Yes.

Director: What gets the ones who dread up on their feet?

Friend: It's like we've been saying — hope.

Director: What gets the overly hopeful down on the ground? Dread?

Friend: No, not dread.

Director: What then?

Friend: Hard experience.

7

Director: Have the ones who dread had hard experience? Is that what made them dread in the first place?

Friend: I don't know. I just know they need some hope in order to stand up.

Director: What is hope?

Friend: I would say it's the feeling that things are going to be alright.

Director: How do the ones who dread come to that feeling?

Friend: I think I have a metaphor that will help.

Director: What is it?

Friend: They, the ones who dread, get a simple spark of luck, and light a candle with it right away.

Director: The light will give them hope?

Friend: The light is their hope.

Director: But what's the candle?

Friend: Faith.

Director: What's the difference between hope and faith?

Friend: If the light goes out, you still have your candle — and you know it might one day be possible to light it up again. You only need that tiny spark.

Win

Persons of the Dialogue

Director

Friend

1

Director: What does it mean to win?

Friend: To be the best.

Director: What else?

Friend: To defeat your opponents.

Director: Anything else?

Friend: I think that covers it.

Director: What about to win in the sense of winning friends?

Friend: Oh, right — that, too.

Director: Do you like to win?

Friend: Who doesn't?

Director: Do you love to win?

Friend: I'm not that competitive — even concerning friends. Why do you ask?

Director: I'm wondering about something someone said to me.

Friend: What?

Director: He said I always have to win the argument.

Friend: Do you?

2

Director: What does it mean to win an argument?

Friend: I think it's one of a few things. One, you might reduce the other side to silence. Two, you might win the person over to your point of view. Three, the person might remain unmoved but you might win the witnesses to the argument over to your side.

Director: But don't I win, too, if I am persuaded to come over to the other person's point of view?

Friend: How do you figure?

Director: That would involve my learning something, wouldn't it?

Friend: I suppose.

Director: And learning something is a win, isn't it — winning a prize?

Friend: Many people aren't going to see it that way.

Director: What do I care what many people think as long as it's the truth?

Friend: They'll say you lost the argument.

Director: The only way to lose an argument is to fail to follow where it leads.

Friend: By lose, you mean to lose its trail.

Director: Yes.

Friend: People just don't see it that way, Director.

3

Director: Because they want philosophy to be competitive?

Friend: That's right.

Director: But it's not competitive. To make it competitive is to pervert it.

Friend: Because philosophy is a search for truth?

Director: Don't you think it is?

Friend: I don't know. A lot of people see that claim to search for truth as a smoke screen for competitive behavior.

Director: Philosophers want to be the alpha male?

Friend: That's how it seems in a lot of cases.

Director: I'll tell you how it seems to me. When people engage in philosophic dialogue they should be striving to win the other over as a friend, in a friendship based on sharing the truth.

Friend: What if they are already friends?

Director: Then they try to find the truth together.

Friend: And if they find it they've won?

Director: Yes, that round of the bout, at least.

Friend: Is that all philosophy is, finding truth?

Director: No. It's about more than that.

Friend: What's it about?

4

Director: It's about the love of wisdom, and it's about the attempt to replace opinion with knowledge.

Friend: And if you replace someone else's opinion with your knowledge, you've won?

Director: If you do, it's a win-win situation — for gaining knowledge is a win, remember?

Friend: But it's your knowledge they are gaining.

Director: My knowledge? Knowledge doesn't belong to anyone. I just showed my interlocutor where the knowledge is.

Friend: What kind of knowledge do you argue about?

Director: Me? I tend not to argue about, tend not to have dialogue about, natural science. I am more interested in what I will call the human things.

Friend: What are the human things?

Director: Virtues, for one.

Friend: Isn't winning a virtue?

Director: It can also be a vice.

Friend: How?

Director: If, for instance, you are so bent on confounding your interlocutor in an argument that you fail to listen carefully to what he is saying, you have lost, in terms of virtue, even if you reduce him to silence.

Friend: But everyone else will think you've won.

Director: Not everyone, necessarily.

5

Friend: How else can winning be a vice?

Director: It can be if you focus on winning to the exclusion of other, appropriate virtues.

Friend: Can you give me an example?

Director: Sure. Suppose you forget about politeness, kindness, and simple humanity in the course of striving to win. Victory, in such a case, would be vicious, no?

Friend: You have a point.

Director: We could say more about the virtues of fairness, sportsmanship, humility, and the like, couldn't we?

Friend: We certainly could. It seems that the drive to win can crowd out other virtues.

Director: Yes. But is there a time when that is not so?

Friend: I'm not sure. Is there?

Director: What about the drive to win friends? Can that be taken too far?

Friend: I think it can. You might become obnoxious to the people you are trying to win over.

Director: So you have to have some sort of knowledge that tells you when you are about to go too far?

Friend: I think you do. But what knowledge is that?

Director: A knowledge of people. While trying to win someone over you have to watch how he reacts and pick up on clues.

6

Friend: What are these clues?

Director: Impatience, irritation, boredom, and so on.

Friend: So if you see those signs you stop trying to win him over?

Director: At least for the moment. You might fall back and try regrouping in order to make another attempt later on.

Friend: What's most likely to win a friend over — showing his way to knowledge, or saying things that resonate with him?

Director: I don't see the difference that clearly, Friend. To me, knowledge is what resonates most.

Friend: Because the knowledge is already in us?

Director: That's the best kind of knowledge.

Friend: This is knowledge of our human things, our virtue?

Director: Yes.

Friend: So you, in the course of trying to win a friend over, show him what his virtues are.

Director: That's my hope.

Friend: But that means you also show him what his virtues aren't.

Director: That's the obverse side of the coin, yes.

Friend: If someone thinks magnanimity is his greatest virtue, and you show him that it isn't, is he likely to become your friend?

7

Director: If he's not really magnanimous, he may have a hard time adjusting. So he may not be my friend at once. It may take some time for him to come around.

Friend: But if you show someone that he is brave when he thinks himself to be a coward, he likely wouldn't need any time to come around, right?

Director: That seems likely.

Friend: So when you win your friends over, do they mostly come around at once or do they mostly take time?

Director: You're asking me if I mostly inflate or deflate the egos of my potential friends?

Friend: Yes.

Director: It's a hard question because sometimes I do both.

Friend: Can you give me an example of that?

Director: Suppose someone is dishonest but brave, but thinks himself honest but cowardly. I praise his bravery and censure, blame, his dishonesty. How does that affect him? It's hard to say. He may be proud enough of being thought to be brave that he can work on his dishonesty while being a friend to me. But he may be so ashamed of his dishonesty that he has to go away for a while to work on it alone.

Friend: Do you consider it a win if he has to go away?

Director: Is doing what you feel you have to do winning? If yes, then the man in question has won.

Friend: But what about you? Have you won?

Director: Often times I don't know. The score, if this can be likened to a game, is delayed in reaching me.

GUT

Persons of the Dialogue

Director

Friend

1

Friend: I should have listened to my gut.

Director: Don't be too hard on yourself. Why didn't you?

Friend: I didn't think I had a choice.

Director: Why?

Friend: Because I thought it would be unreasonable to listen to my gut.

Director: But why?

Friend: Because your gut can be wrong at times.

Director: How can your gut be wrong? It simply is what it is.

Friend: Well, sometimes necessity doesn't allow you to listen to your gut.

Director: You're forced to go against your gut?

Friend: Sometimes, yes. Choice is a luxury.

Director: Tell me more about how your gut can be wrong.

Friend: What is your gut? It's made up of your past experiences and the intuition you develop from them, right?

Director: Yes, and I'd add that what you think, or how you feel, about your past experiences also plays a part.

Friend: What if you come into a new situation that has some superficial similarities to past experience, experience that was bad? Your gut might tell you to stay away, when if you only would look more closely you might see that it is a different situation entirely, one you might enjoy.

2

Director: So you're counseling to trust your gut but verify?

Friend: Yes, exactly. As you look into the situation you're already on alert for bad signs because of what your gut said.

Director: So the only problem then would be if in the process of looking more closely you commit yourself to something you might not want to be committed to, right?

Friend: Exactly. The more you learn the greater, at times, are the expectations that you will do what you are looking into doing.

Director: So you have to be brave enough to look more closely and strong enough to go against expectations if it turns out your gut was right.

Friend: Yes.

Director: Let's suppose you sign up for this new venture, or whatever it is you're looking into. Won't the things your gut objected to initially still be there and still irritate?

Friend: They will.

Director: So the things you learn about would have to more than make up for that?

Friend: That's right.

Director: But the bothersome things will always be there, underneath it all, ironically enough, considering that you saw them on the surface right away.

Friend: Yes, it is ironic. I guess this is where necessity comes in. You know certain things are going to bother you but you feel you don't have a choice.

Director: I'm not going to say you always have a choice, because sometimes you don't. So what do you do if you have to go against your gut?

Friend: You suck it up and do it, as they say.

3

Director: Can you try to do anything about the things that bother you?

Friend: What can you do? Usually the things that bother your gut have to do with the totality of the situation.

Director: The totality of the situation? You mean you take it all in at first glance?

Friend: Yes. I believe we all do this. The first impression is very important.

Director: But first impressions can be wrong?

Friend: This is where I'm torn. On the one hand, I believe that first impressions are always right — your gut is always right. On the other hand, I wonder what happens to someone who is bigoted or prejudiced about a situation. Is his first impression right?

Director: Maybe it is for him.

Friend: But shouldn't he learn to go against his prejudices?

Director: Are you prejudiced, Friend?

Friend: I don't know. What if I am and I don't know it?

Director: And you're saying that one way to find out if you are is to go against your gut, because your gut might consist of prejudices, and see if you were wrong?

Friend: Yes.

Director: Why not question to see what prejudices you might have first, before you have to put your gut to the test? That way when you do have to put it to the test, you are free to listen to your gut, to the extent that necessity might not force you otherwise. And even in that case, in being forced, your gut has given you fair warning of what might be likely to come — an advantage.

Friend: How do I test myself for prejudices?

4

Director: First you should distinguish preference from prejudice. It's fine to have preferences. And it's fine for your gut to warn you that a certain situation might go against some or many of your preferences.

Friend: I never thought about it that way before, gut consisting of preferences.

Director: Now what about prejudices?

Friend: I'm not sure.

Director: Well, what is a prejudice?

Friend: It's irrational.

Director: Why?

Friend: Because you've made up your mind before you have the facts.

Director: But your gut reaction is precisely reaction to the facts, isn't it?

Friend: Yes, but you might not have all of the facts.

Director: When does one get all of the facts?

Friend: Usually when you've committed yourself to a certain course. That's when the full truth comes out.

Director: If something seems bad on the surface, is it likely to be bad in the depths?

Friend: I don't know.

Director: Nonetheless, the superficial things will have some impact on you, no?

Friend: That's true.

5

Director: Can the surface seem good but the depths be bad?

Friend: Of course.

Director: What's harder to be good at, the surface or the depths?

Friend: I would say the depths.

Director: So some people might be likely to make their surface look good in order to cover up a deficiency in the depths?

Friend: Very likely, I would say.

Director: Then what would a bad surface tell you?

Friend: That the depths are likely rotten.

Director: What does your gut sense most, the surface or the depths?

Friend: The surface.

Director: So if it reacts negatively to a bad surface, doesn't it seem like a good idea to listen to it?

Friend: Yes, it does.

Director: Even though you haven't got all of the facts.

Friend: Even so.

6

Director: And suppose it turns out that you were wrong, that a certain course of action seemed bad on the surface but was great in the depths. Would you have acted out of prejudice, or out of good sense based on what's likely for most situations?

Friend: Good sense. But that, you know, is what I'm always afraid of.

Director: Acting out of good sense?

Friend: No, missing the diamond in the rough, as they say.

Director: How can you find that diamond without committing yourself to what likely is a bad course?

Friend: I'm not sure I can. It's a risk.

Director: Do rough diamonds give off signs that your gut can pick up on?

Friend: They might.

Director: Have you ever found something good in the depths of what, on the surface, was a bad situation?

Friend: I have.

Director: Were there signs beforehand that you might recognize again?

Friend: No, not that I'm aware of. I think it was just luck in that case.

Director: Are you as likely to have luck someplace good as you are someplace bad?

Friend: Probably even more likely.

Director: Then why are you so down? Listen when your gut tells you that someplace, or something, is bad or good.

Ignore

Persons of the Dialogue

Director

Friend

1

Director: What does it mean to ignore someone?

Friend: To take no notice, to pay no attention to him.

Director: Why would you ignore someone?

Friend: Because he is not a positive force in your life.

Director: What does it mean to be a positive force?

Friend: Some people amplify your energy, and some people drain your energy. The former are the positive, and the latter are the negative.

Director: So you simply ignore the negative.

Friend: That's right.

Director: Do the negative ones like being ignored?

Friend: No. It drives some of them crazy.

Director: Why do you think that is?

Friend: I don't know.

Director: They can't drain you unless you pay attention to them?

Friend: No, they can't.

Director: How exactly do they drain you?

Friend: They make everything difficult for you.

2

Director: And they harvest energy from this effort of theirs?

Friend: I'm not sure they harvest any energy.

Director: So the energy just dissipates?

Friend: Yes.

Director: Then why do they bother?

Friend: Maybe they just can't stand to see the positive.

Director: And energy is a positive.

Friend: Of course.

Director: And when positive meets positive the energies enhance, or amplify, one another?

Friend: Yes.

Director: What happens when a positive meets a neutral?

Friend: Why, nothing, I suppose.

Director: So there's no harm in neutrals.

Friend: None that I can see.

Director: So you wouldn't ignore a neutral?

Friend: Well, you might. I mean, there'd be no reason not to, right?

3

Director: What if the neutrals can warn you about negatives? Wouldn't that be worth paying attention to?

Friend: I suppose it would. But why would the neutrals know more about the negatives than the positives?

Director: They can come in contact with the negatives without being drained. So they tend to know more about the negatives than the positives.

Friend: So positives shouldn't ignore the neutrals.

Director: That's how it seems to me. But tell me something, Friend. Are the negatives jealous of the energy of the positives? Is that really all there is to all of this?

Friend: Sometimes I think that's exactly it.

Director: So we should ignore those who are jealous of us.

Friend: I can't think of anything else to do with them. Attacking them is only a bigger waste of energy.

Director: Is it difficult to ignore them?

Friend: At first it is. But I think it gets easier with time.

Director: Why?

Friend: At first they still come around to bother you. But over time they tend to forget about you.

Director: And when they at first come around to bother you, what do they do that makes it difficult to ignore them?

4

Friend: They taunt you and provoke you.

Director: Why is it hard to ignore that?

Friend: Because they often know of a sore spot to press.

Director: A sore spot from how you interacted with them?

Friend: Yes.

Director: Tell me more about this sore spot.

Friend: It's usually something you did that you somewhat regret. Not that it was something wrong. A sympathetic observer would have no problem with it. But it was something you did that could have been done better.

Director: And it bothers you that you could have done it better?

Friend: Yes.

Director: So the negatives prey on this feeling of yours.

Friend: They do.

Director: It's the only hold they have on your attention?

Friend: It is.

Director: Then you have to deny them that hold.

Friend: How do you do that?

5

Director: You have to let go of worry about what you could have done better.

Friend: But here's the problem. This thing that you did, it gets to your core sense of yourself.

Director: Your core sense of yourself? Tell me more about this.

Friend: Suppose you think of yourself as an essentially reasonable person. But you do something that might be taken as unreasonable, depending on who you ask. The negatives intuit that you think of yourself as an essentially reasonable person and press the attack precisely on this questionable action.

Director: What if you were really unreasonable? Would that be the end of the world?

Friend: It would be a very difficult thing to swallow and digest.

Director: But if you do swallow and digest it, won't you be the stronger for it?

Friend: I guess.

Director: Isn't it better to swallow and digest it than to spend energy defending yourself from the negatives?

Friend: I suppose.

Director: And wouldn't the negatives be shocked that you were able to do this?

Friend: You know, I think they would be.

Director: Now suppose you only have something questionable to swallow and digest, not something fully against your core sense of yourself. Wouldn't that be easier?

Friend: Yes, I think it would.

Director: And wouldn't it madden the negatives?

Friend: Very much so.

6

Director: So what do you do if ever you have a sore spot that they press?

Friend: Take that sore spot away from them — and then ignore them. But this is easier said than done.

Director: What's so hard about it?

Friend: You always want to feel you are in the right.

Director: Isn't it right to own up to your own questionable actions and mistakes?

Friend: It is.

Director: And how do you own up to them?

Friend: You swallow and digest them.

Director: So there's nothing else to be done, right?

Friend: But maybe you can make up for your mistakes, your questionable actions.

Director: How?

Friend: You come on even stronger in your core values, reasonableness in this case.

Director: Being reasonable with the negatives? But that's the trap they set for you. They want you to feel like that, that you should come on stronger. They want you to be hyper-reasonable with them. They're counting on it. No, you have to digest your questionable action and turn away from these people or they will bleed you dry.

Friend: I think you're right. But what if we change the metaphor up?

Director: What do you mean?

7

Friend: What if instead of positives, neutrals, and negatives we have something else?

Director: Like what?

Friend: The interesting and the uninteresting.

Director: Let me guess. We pay attention to the interesting and ignore the uninteresting.

Friend: Exactly. What do you think?

Director: What harm is there in paying attention to the uninteresting?

Friend: You waste time you could be spending with the interesting.

Director: So now we're talking about time instead of energy.

Friend: Yes.

Director: Well, I think this makes sense. But how do the uninteresting make claims on your time?

Friend: They prey, like the negatives, on your core values.

Director: Like being polite and accommodating?

Friend: Right.

Director: And the uninteresting are attracted to the interesting?

Friend: Of course.

8

Director: But now you know what the problem is, don't you?

Friend: What problem?

Director: Different people will find different people interesting.

Friend: Why is that a problem?

Director: We won't be able to say whether someone is simply uninteresting. We will only be able to say someone is uninteresting, to me.

Friend: That's not a problem.

Director: Is it a problem for the other metaphor?

Friend: You mean we can only say that someone is a negative, for me?

Director: Yes. Is that more problematic?

Friend: I need to think about that because some negatives, I think, are simply negative — for everyone.

Director: For everyone.

Friend: Like I said, I need to think about it.

Director: Well, while you're thinking about it, tell me — is the remedy the same for the uninteresting as for the negative?

Friend: The remedy's the same. Swallow, digest, ignore.

Director: And is the remedy for the negative the same no matter whether a negative is a negative for everyone, or only for you?

Friend: The remedy remains the same whenever someone preys upon your weaknesses. Of this I'm sure.

Persons of the Dialogue

Director

Magician

Friend

1

Magician: Of course I hide.

Friend: But why?

Magician: Why? Because I don't want to be found.

Friend: But who are you hiding from?

Magician: People I don't want to see.

Friend: Why don't you want to see them?

Magician: Because they know my tricks.

Director: They know your tricks?

Magician: Yes.

Director: Are you talking about your magic tricks, or some other kind of tricks?

Magician: Well, honestly? The other kind of tricks.

Friend: What are these other tricks?

Magician: I suppose it would be simplest to call them lies.

Friend: You're a liar?

Magician: Yes.

Friend: What sorts of lies do you tell?

Magician: Oh, all sorts.

Friend: Give us an example.

2

Magician: I lie about what I like.

Friend: What do you mean?

Magician: Suppose you baked an apple pie and served it to me covered with vanilla ice cream.

Director: Are you going to say you'd eat the ice cream and pie even though you don't like ice cream on your pie?

Magician: How did you know?

Director: A lucky guess.

Friend: But that's not a bad lie.

Magician: But what if you tell little lies like that all the time? They add up, you know.

Friend: They add up to so much that you feel compelled to hide from people?

Magician: Yes — when people come to sense that I've been lying.

Friend: Well that seems sort of pathetic, Magician, I'm sorry to say.

Magician: Don't be sorry about the truth, my friend.

Friend: Do you tell other lies?

Magician: On occasion, like anyone, I suppose. But those lies about what I like are the problem.

Friend: Why don't you just start telling the truth?

Magician: I can't stand the thought of letting people down.

3

Friend: You're a people pleaser?

Magician: In the worst way.

Friend: Director, what do you think about this?

Director: I think Magician isn't telling us the whole story.

Friend: You mean it's not just about little lies as to what he likes?

Director: I think there is one big lie behind all of the little lies.

Friend: What?

Director: Would you care to tell us, Magician?

Magician: I have no idea what you're talking about. What lie?

Director: I'll start with the truth. You don't like very many people. In fact, there are very, very few people you genuinely like. But you're a performer, and you feel you can't afford to alienate people. So you tell lots of little lies to make things go better. The big lie is that you like the people you're lying to.

Magician: You've got me. But what am I to do? I have to deal with people.

Friend: Just be yourself. You don't have to like everyone. Just be polite to them.

Magician: But people don't feel that's enough. They want you to be friendly with them, too. They expect it.

Friend: What's wrong with being friendly?

Magician: That's where my lies start, precisely there.

4

Director: Friend, what happens, with many people, if you are polite to them without being friendly?

Friend: They think you're stuck up.

Director: What does it mean to be stuck up?

Friend: To think you're better than others.

Director: Do you think you are better than others, Magician?

Magician: I'm a better magician. But as a person, simply? No, of course not. In fact, it seems to me that most people are better than I am.

Director: Better at being friendly?

Magician: Ah, you caught me. Yes, that is what I was thinking.

Friend: And you don't think it's good to be friendly?

Magician: It's no good to be friendly to everyone. Why should you be? You should be friendly to people you like. Don't you think I'm friendly with you two?

Friend: I think you are.

Director: Friendliness aside, tell us, Magician — did you become a magician in order to get away from people?

Magician: Why, yes. I'm all alone when I'm on stage.

Director: And it's when you're not on stage that things get difficult.

Magician: Yes.

Friend: So is your solution to be on stage as much as possible?

Magician: You are very perceptive, Friend.

5

Friend: But then when you're not working, what do you do?

Magician: I garden. I cook. I read.

Friend: And you do all of these things alone.

Magician: Yes.

Friend: So when do you see people, aside from those in your audience?

Magician: You know how things are. I have certain professional obligations that bring me in contact with certain nice people.

Friend: Are you being sarcastic when you say "nice"?

Magician: No, I mean it. They seem nice.

Director: Nice, but not for you?

Magician: Exactly.

Friend: But I don't believe you really think they are nice.

Magician: Why not?

Friend: Because if you thought they were nice you would want to spend time with them — they would be "for you."

Magician: Ah, Friend. There's something you don't understand. I don't think that I, myself, am nice.

Friend: You think you're mean?

Magician: Maybe "rotten" is a better word.

6

Friend: But what's rotten about you?

Magician: I notice all sorts of things about people, not very nice things.

Friend: But are these the people you think are nice?

Magician: Yes.

Friend: But that doesn't make any sense. You think they are nice but notice things that are not very nice about them?

Magician: I understand your perplexity. But that's the way of it.

Friend: Why not just think these people aren't nice?

Magician: Because then I'll be stuck believing that nobody is nice, truly nice.

Friend: Not even Director and me?

Magician: I'm afraid if I allow myself to look at you the way I look at others that's the conclusion I'll come to.

Friend: So what do you do, close your eyes when you're with us?

Magician: Metaphorically, yes.

Friend: But that's crazy.

Director: That's how it is, Friend, when you're trying to protect a belief you don't believe wholeheartedly, in this case that there are indeed nice people in the world.

Magician: But I'm afraid of what will happen to me if I stop believing.

Friend: I'll tell you what will happen to you — you'll become bitter.

7

Magician: Bitter and rotten. Just my luck.

Director: I'm not at all sure you're rotten, my friend. And it's not at all clear you'll become bitter. But I do think you need to do it.

Magician: Look at you two the way I look at everybody else?

Director: Yes.

Magician: But what if I see that you're not very nice, just like the others?

Director: Then you're going to have to do some reconciling.

Magician: Reconciling?

Director: Do you enjoy our company?

Magician: Yes.

Director: Truly?

Magician: Well, I do. But only for so long. Then I want to be alone again.

Friend: Who doesn't like company only for so long? There's nothing odd about that.

Magician: Thank you. But what do I need to reconcile?

Director: The fact that you enjoy our company, for however short a time, with the fact that you find us to be not very nice, if that's what you do indeed think of us.

Magician: Maybe you're like food.

Friend: Like food?

Magician: Yes, you're perishable.

Friend: You mean we're only good for so long.

Magician: Yes. You're nice for a while.

Director: Is that how you feel about other people?

Magician: Yes. But they have a much shorter shelf life than you two — some of them mere seconds.

Director: What do you need to do when the shelf life runs out?

Magician: I need to go, and right away.

Friend: That's where you lie, then, isn't it? You stay longer than you want to.

Magician: Yes. But now I will tell the truth. And the truth is that it's time for me to go! Goodbye!

Rock

Persons of the Dialogue

Director

Friend

1

Director: What does it mean to be like a rock?

Friend: It means you are strong and steady.

Director: Like a foundation stone?

Friend: Yes, exactly — a cornerstone.

Director: I see. But what does it mean to be strong and steady?

Friend: You are unflappable.

Director: An important trait for someone who is, or is to be, a rock.

Friend: Why are you asking about rocks, Director?

Director: Someone told me I am a rock.

Friend: Well, I'm sure he was paying you a compliment.

Director: Why are you so sure about that?

Friend: It's always meant as a compliment.

Director: I don't see how it's always a compliment.

Friend: Why not?

Director: Couldn't someone who is unfeeling be called a rock? After all, rocks
have no feelings, right?

Friend: No, the idea is that you master your feelings. That's what your strength and steadiness are all about.

Director: They're all about mastery of oneself?

Friend: Yes, emphatically.

2

Director: So this person was telling me that I am master of myself.

Friend: I'm sure he was.

Director: But we are all masters of ourselves, are we not?

Friend: However true that may be, we don't all master ourselves equally well.

Director: Suppose I have mastered myself. Is that supposed to make me fit to bear the weight of other rocks?

Friend: Yes, I suppose.

Director: And what am I supposed to do with the weight of all these rocks on top of me?

Friend: Stay strong and steady.

Director: What's the reward for doing so?

Friend: It is an honor to be a foundation stone.

Director: I see. But these rocks atop me, they are not fit, I suppose, to be in my place?

Friend: No, the strongest and steadiest rock is laid as the foundation stone.

Director: Then what are they that I should support them?

Friend: What do you mean?

Director: Should the strongest and most steady support the weaker and less steady?

Friend: You're asking why you would want to do this?

Director: Yes. What's in it for me except the honor?

3

Friend: Are you saying honor has no value?

Director: Of course I'm not. I'm just trying to see what is involved in this being a rock business.

Friend: Well, aside from the honor, I think you'll find that once you're locked into place you have no choice but to be strong and steady.

Director: Why is that an advantage to be sought?

Friend: Because if you're not locked into place you might be tempted to waiver.

Director: Ah, this is about fighting temptation.

Friend: Yes.

Director: But if I had not been good at fighting temptation, I would not have been chosen as the foundation stone, now would I?

Friend: That's true.

Director: You seem to be saying that it must come as a relief to be free of temptation, once locked into place.

Friend: Yes.

Director: So we have honor and release from temptation as rewards. But I see a problem.

Friend: What problem?

4

Director: What if I am tantalized by things I can never have, things that approach me in my corner of the foundation? Might that not be enough to drive me mad?

Friend: I don't see how. You know you can't have them.

Director: Yes, but before I became a foundation stone I could take pride in resisting temptation. In my new role that pride would be gone, would it not?

Friend: No, it would only be replaced by the pride you'll feel in supporting the whole structure.

Director: That reminds me — what sort of structure will this be?

Friend: Why should that matter?

Director: Why should that matter? Oh, Friend! Doesn't it matter? Do all buildings deserve to stand strong? What if I am the cornerstone to the palace of a wicked king? Does that not matter?

Friend: Well, you're going to have to learn to live with this, Director. The occupants of buildings change many times throughout the life of the structure.

Director: You're telling me I have to learn to live with supporting evil?

Friend: If it comes to it, yes.

Director: I cannot do this, Friend. I will only support good.

Friend: But once you're locked in you'll have no choice.

Director: Of course I will. I will stop being strong and steady rather than serve evil.

Friend: But everything will fall down on top of you!

Director: I am strong enough for that.

5

Friend: So you won't really stop being strong. You'll just stop being steady.

Director: Yes, now that you mention it, that's exactly what I'll be — strong, but unsteady.

Friend: You know, if you do that once, no one will ever, ever, want to use you again as a foundation stone.

Director: I suppose that's the price I pay. If I can't support good, then let me support nothing. But will it really come to that, Friend?

Friend: What do you mean?

Director: Aren't there people out there, good people, who would rather that their palace topple than be put to use by evil ones?

Friend: Yes, I think you have a point. You will always be prized as a cornerstone by the good who do not wish to see their structure put to evil use.

Director: Maybe I can get the hang of being a rock after all. But tell me, Friend, what is it that makes me strong?

Friend: You have the courage of your convictions.

Director: Courage makes me strong?

Friend: Yes.

Director: And what of my convictions? What do you think they are?

Friend: You believe in fairness, honesty, decency, and kindness.

Director: If I were unfair, dishonest, indecent, and unkind you wouldn't say I'm strong?

Friend: Well, I don't know.

Director: You don't know? Why?

6

Friend: Evil can be strong, too, depending.

Director: Depending on what?

Friend: Depending on how much support it garners.

Director: Who supports the unfair?

Friend: Those who have no care for fairness.

Director: Who supports the dishonest?

Friend: Those who have no care for honesty.

Director: And so on with those who have no care for decency and kindness?

Friend: Yes.

Director: Can any effort succeed with none of these virtues?

Friend: I'm afraid it can.

Director: What have the ones engaged in such an effort got in common?

Friend: An evil end.

Director: Such as the construction of a great structure to their glory?

Friend: Yes, precisely. But now I've thought of something.

Director: What?

7

Friend: You should be their foundation stone.

Director: Why, so I can become unsteady once the structure is complete, to bring it all toppling down?

Friend: Yes, exactly! Just imagine. One person's efforts alone could bring down a formidable castle of evil. One alone!

Director: But now I wonder, Friend. Would I be too locked into place to do it alone? Wouldn't I have to persuade the adjacent stones to become unstable, too?

Friend: You might be right. And who better to persuade them than you?

Director: Ah, now we're saying I'm not merely a rock after all, no? For rocks are not known for their ability to persuade.

Friend: That's true.

Director: So I only seem to be a rock.

Friend: Right.

Director: And those around me, once I'm locked into place, they, too, cannot be rocks, can they? I mean, are rocks open to persuasion?

Friend: No, they're not.

Director: So we need many like me in place to bring the evil structure down.

Friend: We do.

Director: What are we seeming rocks properly called?

Friend: Philosophers.

Persons of the Dialogue

Director

Friend

1

Director: What is doubt, Friend?

Friend: An unwillingness to believe something is true.

Director: What do you doubt?

Friend: Just about everything.

Director: Why?

Friend: Because most everything seems doubtful to me.

Director: What doesn't seem doubtful to you?

Friend: Our friendship, for one — as much as it's possible not to doubt something.

Director: What makes our friendship special?

Friend: We both work at it.

Director: Ah, is that the secret then?

Friend: What do you mean?

Director: The secret to believing, to certainty, is work.

Friend: You know, it just might be.

2

Director: Don't scientists work to obtain certainty?

Friend: They do.

Director: But is their certainty different than the sort of certainty among two friends?

Friend: It is. Their certainty doesn't involve a human relationship.

Director: And human relationships are more complicated than what scientists work with?

Friend: Infinitely so.

Director: What doubts can there be in human relationships?

Friend: Oh, many.

Director: Name one.

Friend: You can doubt the other's veracity.

Director: What else?

Friend: You can doubt his intentions.

Director: Anything else?

Friend: You can doubt his good faith.

Director: How do you stop these doubts?

Friend: You engage in dialogue that reassures you.

Director: Dialogue can bring you to certainty?

Friend: As close to certainty as it is possible to come.

3

Director: What if you have a friend who is a really good liar?

Friend: Then I suppose that I am a fool.

Director: Because you believe him.

Friend: Yes.

Director: So in order not to be a fool you might simply never believe.

Friend: Yes, you can always doubt, in any relationship.

Director: But isn't that doubt like a cancer in the relationship?

Friend: That's precisely the problem.

Director: At a certain point you simply have to trust.

Friend: Yes.

Director: How do you know when you've reached that point?

Friend: I'm not sure you can actually know for certain.

Director: You take a leap of faith?

Friend: Yes, exactly.

Director: And this leap is either rewarded or punished accordingly.

Friend: Yes. But you really have to make the leap. You can't go about it half-heartedly.

Director: You have to be willing to risk it, without hedging your bets?

Friend: That's right.

4

Director: What exactly are you risking?

Friend: Why, your heart, Director.

Director: You open your heart to your friend.

Friend: You do.

Director: And a doubting heart can't open fully.

Friend: No, it cannot.

Director: But what if your friend doesn't open his heart to you? Would you be able to tell?

Friend: I think so. An open heart can generally sense whether another heart is also open, or not. But this is why you probe and don't open up all at once.

Director: So this is something of a dance, then, isn't it? You open your heart a bit. Your friend opens his a bit more. You meet his bit more and open yours a bit further. Your friend closes his a touch, and you do the same. And so on.

Friend: Yes, becoming friends involves a dance of hearts.

Director: But then is there no more dancing once fully friends?

Friend: You mean once both hearts are fully open?

Director: Yes. Or do the hearts not stay fully open? Don't doubts always creep back in?

Friend: Doubts most certainly do creep their way back in.

Director: So the dance must go on.

Friend: The dance must go on.

5

Director: Someone with lots of friends does lots of dancing, I suppose.

Friend: Yes.

Director: Does his heart get tired from it all?

Friend: It does.

Director: Would it be easier instead to have a handful of truly close friends?

Friend: Not necessarily.

Director: Why not?

Friend: You might dance indifferently with friends that aren't very close. But close friends demand everything you've got. While the dancing with them can be exhilarating, it can also be exhausting.

Director: The closer the friend the better the dance?

Friend: Many times, yes. But sometimes this is not so.

Director: Why not?

Friend: Sometimes friends aren't very good dancers. They rush in and open their hearts fully.

Director: And then they expect the same of you.

Friend: Yes. Can you see how that would be very taxing if you're not ready to open up fully?

Director: I think I can. So you prefer good dancers for your friends.

Friend: Ideally, yes.

Director: And by dancing, we mean both the opening and the closing of the heart to the other.

Friend: We do.

6

Director: Is there a dance where two people start with wide open hearts, as much as that is possible, and slowly dance and close their hearts completely?

Friend: There is.

Director: What kind of dance is that?

Friend: It's a sad dance. It's the dance of the end of a friendship.

Director: But can't the two dancers start up another dance at another time and open their hearts back up, renew the friendship?

Friend: It's possible, but it is rare.

Director: Why?

Friend: Because people don't usually end a friendship like that unless one or both of their hearts have been wounded deeply.

Director: And an open heart is most easily wounded?

Friend: Yes.

Director: Is that why people doubt others, to protect their hearts?

Friend: That's the main reason.

Director: So some healthy doubt might save a friendship?

Friend: Perhaps. But some friendships are doomed from the start. What might be saved by some healthy doubt is a heart from wounding.

Director: Because doubt is a sort of armor for the heart.

Friend: Yes.

7

Director: What about for the mind?

Friend: What do you mean?

Director: Is doubt a virtue of the mind?

Friend: Yes, I think it is.

Director: What is good about it?

Friend: It helps sift out the truth.

Director: Because doubt is a form of scrutiny.

Friend: Exactly.

Director: But if you doubt almost everything here, too, Friend, how do you know you're not wrongly doubting what is in fact the truth?

Friend: Maybe you have to take a leap of faith, as with the heart.

Director: The truth involves faith? I thought truth involves knowledge.

Friend: What is knowledge but something you believe to be true?

Director: Yes, but don't you need proof?

Friend: Yes, of course you do. But you have to believe in the proof, too.

Director: So you're saying that everything in the mind involves faith?

Friend: I am.

8

Director: But if everything is a matter of faith, then everything, too, can be a matter of doubt, no?

Friend: Yes.

Director: So we can go from one extreme to the other — doubt to faith, and faith to doubt?

Friend: We can.

Director: And is this a sort of dance, too?

Friend: Yes, I think it is.

Director: But it's a dance we do only by ourselves?

Friend: No, I think it's a dance we can do with our friends, too.

Director: So we dance to open both heart and mind to friends.

Friend: Yes.

Director: Which involves more risk in the opening, heart or mind?

Friend: I'd say they involve about equal risk.

Director: I understand how a heart is wounded, but how is a mind wounded?

Friend: That's an interesting question. I don't know. I guess it depends on what we mean by mind.

Director: What if mind is belief? Can you be wounded or damaged in what you believe?

Friend: Yes, I suppose you can — assuming it's not a false belief in question. You won't believe it anymore.

9

Director: Now, doesn't the heart have its own beliefs — nay, its own knowing — too?

Friend: I think it does. And now we seem to be at the place where heart meets mind.

Director: Yes. Does heart doubt mind, and mind doubt heart?

Friend: That's a very good question. If either, or both, doubts the other, then I think we have problems.

Director: Heart and mind should be open to one another?

Friend: Emphatically.

Director: Why would the heart close itself off from the mind?

Friend: Maybe the mind is full of poison.

Director: And why would the mind close itself off from the heart?

Friend: Because of poison in the heart.

Director: Can dancing, heart with mind, be the antidote in either case?

Friend: I think it has to be.

Director: Which comes first, this internal, purifying dance, or dancing with others?

Friend: I think you should have yourself in good shape first, before dancing with others.

Director: How many people do you think have themselves in good shape before they take on others?

Friend: Not very many. You can't help but take on others, even though you're not ready, not unless you go and live as a hermit.

Director: Then, short of that, and assuming that we have at least a trace of poison in our hearts and minds, from whatever source, we are always dancing, with ourselves, and others, too.

SPARK

Persons of the Dialogue

Director

Friend

1

Director: So what do you strike together to create a spark in the soul?

Friend: I suppose it could be any two parts of it.

Director: Like heart and mind?

Friend: Sure.

Director: How do you make them strike against one another?

Friend: I think it just happens sometimes.

Director: You mean you can't control it?

Friend: Right.

Director: Will there be a spark if either of these objects, heart and mind, are soft?

Friend: Soft things typically don't spark when struck, no.

Director: So they have to be hard in order to spark.

Friend: Yes, hard headed, and hard hearted — at least during the striking.

Director: Suppose that's the case. What happens when they strike against each other and there is a spark?

Friend: Maybe one or both of them catches on fire.

Director: What would it mean for your heart to be on fire?

Friend: You'd be in lots of pain.

Director: And what if your mind were on fire?

Friend: At the one extreme you would go crazy. At the other extreme you might become a genius.

2

Director: What is it in the heart that burns?

Friend: Sentiments, I guess.

Director: And what is it in the mind that burns?

Friend: Ideas.

Director: Can you say more?

Friend: I suppose ideas are like trees. Some of us have a forest of them. The spark might cause that forest to burn, destroying the trees.

Director: What happens if your forest burns completely down?

Friend: Madness.

Director: How does genius figure into all of this?

Friend: A mind on fire, actively on fire, is genius.

Director: So in order to be an enduring genius you have to have a controlled and constant fire?

Friend: Yes. That's the difference between the genius and the madman. The madman's fire rages out of control, burns the whole forest down, and then goes out.

Director: How does the genius control the fire?

Friend: He digs a trench around it, one it can't cross.

Director: I see. But what fuels the fire after the original trees burn down?

Friend: The genius keeps on bringing fuel — ideas — into the burning zone.

Director: And watches them burn.

Friend: Yes.

3

Director: What if he finds a particularly nice idea, a particularly nice tree? Does he burn it up like the rest?

Friend: That's a good question. No. He sets this tree aside and plants it in a special area of his mind.

Director: Do non-geniuses have special areas like this?

Friend: Some do.

Director: Is the special area of a genius different than that of a non-genius? In other words, is the genius special because of something about his special area?

Friend: His special area is a ring of nice trees surrounding the charred out area in which he burns ideas. Others might have special rings, but they don't have the active burning zone in the middle.

Director: What kind of ideas does the genius burn? False ideas?

Friend: Yes.

Director: And what kind of ideas does he plant in the special ring? True ideas?

Friend: Exactly.

Director: So the genius must know the difference between false and true ideas.

Friend: Yes, he grows quite skilled at differentiating them.

Director: But can't people who are not geniuses know the difference between false and true ideas?

Friend: Well, yes, of course they can.

Director: But the difference is that the genius burns the bad ideas.

Friend: Exactly.

4

Director: What do non-geniuses do with bad ideas?

Friend: Some of them never let the bad ideas into their minds. But some of them do, and then they're hard to get rid of.

Director: The genius has to let the bad ideas in, in order to use them as fuel, no?

Friend: Yes, and that makes him uniquely qualified.

Director: For what?

Friend: To help others whose bad ideas have taken deep root.

Director: How? He starts a fire in their minds?

Friend: Yes.

Director: But how on earth can he do that?

Friend: What if he encourages their heads and hearts to collide?

Director: You said we can't control these collisions. But we can encourage them?

Friend: Yes, let's say we can. The genius might point out contradictions between heart and mind. That will encourage collision.

Director: Are there always contradictions?

Friend: Often enough, yes — especially when bad ideas are involved.

Director: But in order to have a collision that might spark, there must be both a hard heart and a hard head, right?

Friend: I suppose there must, based on what we've been saying.

5

Director: So let's say a collision happens between the hard head and heart. Sparks fly and start a fire in the mind.

Friend: Okay.

Director: How will this fire be controlled? I mean, what if it burns down all of the trees, and not just the bad ones?

Friend: That's the risk.

Director: But can't the genius help control the fire?

Friend: If the person in question is willing to engage in dialogue with him, yes.

Director: And that dialogue can put trenches around the trees that are to be saved from the fire?

Friend: Yes. The dialogue can also bring water to extinguish the fire, depending on what is most appropriate.

Director: Dialogue seems very powerful.

Friend: It is.

Director: Now what of those who cannot, for whatever reason, make head and heart hard, so that no spark is possible? Do they simply never stand in need of fire?

Friend: You mean do only the hard headed and hearted stand in need of fire? I think the answer is no. The others can use some fire now and then, too. So there must be other ways to generate, or catch, a spark.

Director: If there are, wouldn't that mean that geniuses don't necessarily have to start out with hard heads and hearts? Maybe some geniuses started out with heads and hearts that were neither too hard nor too soft. Maybe they were just about right, more or less.

6

Friend: That may be, Director. So what other means do you think there are for sparks, assuming you're not standing close to someone else who is throwing off sparks from his own fire, or that you're not simply struck by lightning, whatever that might mean?

Director: Well, we need two hard things to strike together, right?

Friend: That's what we've been saying.

Director: What can we find in the heart to this end?

Friend: Hard, flinty sentiments. Even a heart that isn't hard overall can have a few of these.

Director: If they strike each other, they might spark?

Friend: Certainly.

Director: What about in the mind?

Friend: Hard ideas.

Director: Ideas not in tree form?

Friend: Yes. We're free to mix the metaphor.

Director: And these ideas, too, might spark if struck together?

Friend: Yes.

Director: And then the fire in the mind might start.

Friend: It might.

7

Director: In either case, heart or mind, what causes the striking?

Friend: The striking is from contradictions.

Director: So you could point out to someone the contradictions within his mind in hope of causing a spark, in further hope of starting a fire. And then, if successful, you could work with him to control the fire.

Friend: Yes, you could. And then he would owe you a debt of gratitude.

Director: Gratitude?

Friend: You are helping him get rid of deeply rooted bad ideas, no? You are helping to burn them out, safely. It's dangerous work, Director. You don't just play with fire. So I'm inclined to say that you deserve some thanks for all you've done.

Time

Persons of the Dialogue

Director

Friend

1

Friend: I have no time.

Director: What? You're young. You have plenty of time.

Friend: That's not what I mean.

Director: What do you mean?

Friend: I mean I have no free time. I'm always working, and then when I'm not working I have other obligations.

Director: What do you want free time for?

Friend: What, are you kidding?

Director: No, I'm not. I mean, why not immerse yourself completely in your work and other obligations and think nothing of it?

Friend: You're assuming that I enjoy my work and other obligations.

Director: You don't?

Friend: No, I don't.

Director: What wrong with your work?

Friend: I'm stressed out all the time.

Director: Why?

Friend: There are so many things that can go wrong, and I have to keep an eye on all of them.

2

Director: Why does that have to be stressful?

Friend: Because I'm not able to keep an eye on all of them, and things go wrong.

Director: So it's your fault that things go wrong, and that's what has you stressed out?

Friend: Yes.

Director: But is it your fault if you've been given more than you can handle?

Friend: I don't know. I guess it depends on whether others would be able to handle it.

Director: If others can do it, it's your fault? If others have the same trouble you do, it's not your fault?

Friend: That sounds about right.

Director: If it's not your fault, if you knew it's not your fault, would you enjoy your time more?

Friend: If I knew? Yes, I guess I would.

Director: Why not bring someone in to substitute for a while and see how he does? Take a leave of absence.

Friend: You're kidding, right? You can't just take a leave like that. And what if that person does a better job? He'll replace me.

Director: Isn't it a better use of your time to be someplace that you belong, someplace where you'll do well, than someplace that you don't belong?

Friend: You mean losing my job would lead to finding a job that's better for me? That sounds nice in theory, but it's hard to lose your job, Director.

Director: Harder than it is to be stressed out all the time?

Friend: Well, I don't know.

3

Director: Suppose you take the leave, or lose your job — what would you do with all of your free time, when not checking in with the old job or looking for a new one?

Friend: I would relax.

Director: What would your relaxation entail?

Friend: Anything I want it to.

Director: Name something.

Friend: Reading.

Director: What would you read?

Friend: Whatever I like.

Director: Have you got anything in mind?

Friend: No. I think I'd just go to the library and browse until something caught my eye.

Director: And this is how you'd spend your day.

Friend: Well, I'd also get some exercise. I think I'd go for nice, long walks.

Director: That sounds pretty good. Anything else?

Friend: I suppose I'd browse the web, watch television — you know.

Director: Would you feel good about your use of your free time?

Friend: Feel good? I'd feel great!

4

Director: But your leave will come to an end, or you'll eventually have to find a new job.

Friend: Yes.

Director: At a minimum, you're looking at forty hours a week.

Friend: That's right.

Director: So it would make sense to find something you like, wouldn't it?

Friend: Yes, but what would I like?

Director: I don't know, Friend. But suppose you find it. If you like it, really like it, is there any reason why you wouldn't want to work more than forty hours a week? Say sixty, or eighty?

Friend: If I really like it? If I love it?

Director: Yes, if you feel like you're thriving on it. Would you still value your free time as much?

Friend: That's an interesting question. If I were really thriving, feeling exhilarated, would I want as much free time? Probably not.

Director: Because what you'd do at work, in this case, would be better than what you'd do with your free time?

Friend: Yes. But I'd still need some down time, in order to rest.

Director: Of course, but you can work that into your schedule from time to time, right?

Friend: Right.

5

Director: Now here's what I'm wondering about. You're having a great time. But someone you have to work closely with is not. He's like what you are now. He does his job, and does it pretty well. But he only wants to work forty hours a week at the maximum, and doesn't enjoy what he's doing. How do you treat him?

Friend: You mean do I treat him as the drag he would be on me?

Director: He would be a drag?

Friend: Of course. He would be a downer.

Director: What would you do?

Friend: I'd replace him if I could, with someone more like me, someone thriving on the work.

Director: You would do this even though you were once like him?

Friend: I'm embarrassed to admit it, but yes, I think I would.

Director: So how would you feel if someone you work for today decided to replace you on similar grounds?

Friend: I'd feel awful. But maybe it would be for the best.

Director: Because it might allow you to find something you love doing?

Friend: That's right. Being let go might allow me to stop serving time at work as though I were in a prison.

Director: So tell me how you would go about finding something you love.

Friend: Well, I, uh, don't know.

6

Director: What do you love doing?

Friend: Reading, going for walks — things like that.

Director: Do you know of any jobs that will allow you to do that?

Friend: Maybe a job as a security guard?

Director: Maybe. Do you want to be a security guard?

Friend: Not really.

Director: Why not?

Friend: I'm afraid I would get bored.

Director: You'd have too much time on your hands?

Friend: Yes, ironically. But I don't really know enough about what security guards do to say for sure. And even if boredom were not a concern, I have financial obligations that require me to earn more than what I think they make.

Director: Forget about the money for a moment. Tell me for certain, now, what it is you really want. More than books. More than walks. Dig down deep inside and say what it is.

Friend: Well, I suppose it really is free time, to do with as I please.

Director: You're sure about that?

Friend: I am.

Director: Then, if that really is the overriding concern, you know what you have to do, don't you?

Friend: Find a well enough paying job in which I only have to work forty hours a week.

Director: Do you think you can do that?

Friend: I don't know.

Director: Why not?

7

Friend: A lot of jobs aren't like that anymore. They expect you to work more hours.

Director: Do they pay you for the extra hours?

Friend: Do they? Of course not.

Director: Then why do people work the extra hours?

Friend: Most people do because it's expected of them.

Director: You mean they'll lose their jobs if they don't.

Friend: Exactly.

Director: Then can't you just find a job that isn't like that?

Friend: The problem is that I am over-qualified, as they say, for most jobs along those lines.

Director: What if you convince them that you really want the job?

Friend: They won't believe me. They'll just think that I'll only be with them until I find something better.

Director: Because it is inconceivable that someone just wants to work forty hours a week, that that is his priority because he values his time too much to spend it on things he doesn't love or enjoy?

Friend: Precisely. They also might think that I'll cause trouble because I think I'm better than the job.

Director: I see. I think I know what you need to do.

Friend: What?

Director: You're going to have to make your own way.

Friend: Blaze my own trail?

Director: Indeed.

Friend: How do I do that?

Director: One difficult step at a time.

Patience

Persons of the Dialogue

Director

Friend

1

Friend: Do you think of yourself as a patient man, Director?

Director: Yes, but not perfectly so.

Friend: What makes you impatient?

Director: People who don't learn.

Friend: What do you think keeps them from learning?

Director: Belief that they already know, when they don't.

Friend: So the first step to learning is knowing that you don't know.

Director: Yes.

Friend: And you are patient with those who know that they don't know.

Director: I am.

Friend: But if they think they know, but don't, you're not.

Director: Not as patient, no.

Friend: You engage people like that?

Director: I do. I try to get them to see that they don't know.

Friend: How do you do that?

Director: Through dialogue.

2

Friend: Such dialogue must take a fair amount of patience, no?

Director: It does. But you have to know how much patience to exercise. I used to exercise near perfect patience with those who think they know, but don't. But I came to see that it's usually a losing proposition to do so. The more patient you are with many of them, the more they feel assured in their ignorance.

Friend: So you just give them a fair chance to come around, and that's it?

Director: I give them more than a fair chance.

Friend: And then you start to lose your patience.

Director: Yes.

Friend: What happens when you do?

Director: I bring the dialogue to an end.

Friend: Just like that?

Director: Just like that.

Friend: Don't you feel bad about ending things abruptly?

Director: Well, I try not to let things get to the point where I am abrupt.

Friend: What do you do?

3

Director: When I feel impatience starting to come on, I immediately take measures to wind down the dialogue gently, before I simply lose my patience and become abrupt.

Friend: Are you generally successful at this?

Director: Generally. But, as you might imagine, I wasn't always so successful.

Friend: Why not?

Director: I didn't know when it was time to give up.

Friend: So you left it up to the others to end the dialogue?

Director: Exactly, even if the dialogue was going nowhere, and showed no sign of ending.

Friend: You held out hope.

Director: Yes, and it was often a misplaced hope.

Friend: Hope is a crucial element of patience, isn't it?

Director: It is, Friend. It doesn't make much sense to be patient unless you have some hope to back it up.

Friend: You hold out hope for those who know that they don't know.

Director: I do.

Friend: And you even hold out some hope for those who think they know, but don't. You must, otherwise you wouldn't bother talking to them.

Director: Yes, I do have some hope for them — but not all that much.

4

Friend: Those who know that they don't know must be patient, no?

Director: Very much so. When you know that you don't know, panic can set in and cause you to lose your patience.

Friend: What happens then?

Director: You rush through everything, grasping at whatever you can, and never really learn anything the way you ought to.

Friend: Do you try to teach patience to someone like that?

Director: I do.

Friend: How?

Director: I try to serve as a model.

Friend: But you already know.

Director: I know some things, but there are a great many things I don't know.

Friend: So you show such people how you approach something that you don't know?

Director: Precisely.

Friend: How do they typically react to that?

Director: They are dismayed at the amount of patience I show.

Friend: They feel like they'll never know what they want to know?

Director: Exactly.

5

Friend: What, in the end, can teach them patience?

Director: Oh, it's rather simple, Friend.

Friend: What?

Director: The realization that there is no other alternative.

Friend: You mean it's impossible to learn without patience.

Director: Yes.

Friend: What happens if they try to learn impatiently?

Director: They'll come to think they know things that they don't know.

Friend: And then you won't have much patience for them anymore.

Director: Right.

Friend: So you're saying that you refuse to have much patience for those who rush.

Director: I am.

Friend: Why do you think people rush?

Director: One simple reason might be that it's very tempting to think you know.

Friend: Why do you think that is?

Director: Maybe the world seems less frightening when you think you do.

6

Friend: Is it less frightening when you actually do know?

Director: I wouldn't know.

Friend: Oh, come on. You do know.

Director: What do I know?

Friend: How the world is.

Director: The world certainly can be scary.

Friend: Yes, but what do you know about the world that calms you, that gives you peace?

Director: About the world? Nothing.

Friend: Are you saying you have no calm, no peace?

Director: No. But my calm and peace don't come from what I know about the world.

Friend: What do they come from?

Director: What I know from my most patient study of all.

Friend: What is the object of this study?

Director: My friends.

Friend: Your friends? You make a study of your friends?

Director: Of course. Don't you?

Friend: Well, no, I don't.

Director: Why not?

Friend: It seems... rude.

7

Director: What's rude about studying your friends in order to know them, really know them?

Friend: I... I don't know. Hey, that's my first step, isn't it?

Director: Yes, I think it is.

Friend: Please try to wipe that grin off of your face.

Director: But I'm happy!

Friend: Happy you got me to admit I don't know something?

Director: Yes. I was worried, you know.

Friend: Worried? About what?

Director: I saw that you thought you knew some of your friends, but really didn't know them.

Friend: Which friends?

Director: Patience, my friend. Patience. You'll know in good time.

Friend: Oh, that's not fair. You already know.

Director: Yes, but you need to come to see these things on your own.

Friend: And there are no shortcuts, I suppose.

Director: No shortcuts. Each shortcut leads you to thinking that you know something that you don't know.

Friend: I wouldn't want you to lose patience with me, so I won't take one.

Director: Are you being sarcastic?

8

Friend: Sarcastic? No. I really don't want you to lose patience with me.

Director: Why do you care if I lose patience with you or not?

Friend: One, you're my good friend and I don't want to lose you. Two, I respect your opinion — or knowledge, I should say — immensely. If you think I need to be patient here, even though I'm dying of curiosity, I will be patient.

Director: I admire you, Friend.

Friend: Why, because I listen to you?

Director: No, because you are showing great command of yourself.

Friend: Thank you. So what do I need to do to start gaining knowledge of my friends?

Director: You need to start wondering if they know what they think they know.

Friend: That's easy. I'm wondering about that now. What do I do next?

Director: Engage them in dialogue.

Friend: To find out what they really know?

Director: Yes.

Friend: But, Director, I've been engaging some of them in dialogue for years. If I don't already know what they know or don't know, what makes you think talking to them now will be any different?

Director: You'll have some help.

Friend: You're going to come with me and talk to them?

Director: Yes, with any of your friends — if you'd like.

Friend: If I'd like? I'd love it! But I'm nervous. What if I don't like what I learn about some of them?

Director: The patient learn to come to terms with what they learn, in time.

FLUFF

Persons of the Dialogue
Director
Friend

1

Director: Fluff? What is fluff?

Friend: You know — something inconsequential.

Director: What in this world of ours is inconsequential?

Friend: Something that doesn't matter.

Director: Something that has no substance? Something that has no weight?

Friend: Exactly. Something that has no impact.

Director: Can you give me an example of something that is fluff?

Friend: I think certain people are fluff.

Director: Is that because they are weak?

Friend: Yes, I suppose. But there seems to be something more to it than that.

Director: What?

Friend: I think they are neither good nor evil.

Director: That's because both good and evil have substance?

Friend: Yes.

Director: Would you rather be good or fluff?

Friend: Good, of course.

Director: Would you rather be evil or fluff?

2

Friend: I knew you were going to ask that.

Director: What would you rather be?

Friend: Fluff, I suppose.

Director: You suppose?

Friend: Fluff gets blown around with the wind.

Director: And you think evil doesn't?

Friend: Evil has its feet planted on the ground.

Director: I don't know, Friend. Isn't evil always hiding or on the run?

Friend: Not always. But at least when evil is on the run, it is in control of where it goes, or where it hides — unlike fluff.

Director: What's so bad about getting blown around with the wind?

Friend: No one will respect you.

Director: Ah, I see. Is evil respected?

Friend: Sometimes.

Director: What about good?

Friend: Good is generally respected — except by evil.

Director: Does fluff respect either good or evil?

Friend: That's a good question. I don't know. It might not be around long enough to bother to respect either of them.

3

Director: But what if there are two types of fluff — domestic and wild?

Friend: The wild lives outdoors in the wind and the domestic lives indoors in the calm?

Director: Yes.

Friend: Maybe the outdoor fluff has no respect for good or evil while the indoor fluff must, of necessity, respect whatever comes its way. After all, it can't just blow away like its outdoor cousin.

Director: And it must respect whatever comes its way because whatever that might be has substance, while it does not?

Friend: That's right.

Director: Is fluff of any use to good or evil?

Friend: I suppose it can serve as a pleasant diversion.

Director: You mean good and evil can pick fluff up in their hands and blow on it and watch it fly?

Friend: Sure. Or they could turn on a fan, and so on.

Director: Is there anything that fluff knows that those with substance wouldn't know?

Friend: Can good and evil learn from fluff? I don't see how.

Director: What about from fluff from the wild?

Friend: Ah, you have a point. Fluff from the wild will have seen many things. Like a fly on the wall, people don't take much notice of fluff, so they speak and act freely before it.

4

Director: Isn't it the same with domestic fluff?

Friend: I suppose it is, now that you mention it — but in a more limited way.

Director: So those of substance can indeed learn something from fluff.

Friend: Yes. But if fluff can retain things to share, doesn't that mean that it is consequential?

Director: What if it retains but doesn't share with good or evil?

Friend: Then I suppose it is inconsequential to them.

Director: But if it shares with someone else, say another fluff, it is consequential to that person?

Friend: Yes.

Director: Isn't that how it is with all things?

Friend: What do you mean?

Director: Something can be consequential in one context or setting, but inconsequential in another.

Friend: Yes, that's true.

Director: So assuming fluff can be consequential to them, and has a choice, with whom would it wish to be consequential — good or evil?

Friend: Well, certainly not with evil.

Director: What good comes of sharing with good?

5

Friend: Fluff can tell good about evil.

Director: To the advantage of good.

Friend: Yes.

Director: Is there a down side to sharing with good?

Friend: Not that I can see.

Director: I see. Say, how will the good think of the fluff? I mean, the fluff will no longer seem to be fluff to the good, right?

Friend: I think the good will think of the fluff as an ally.

Director: An ally that seems to be of substance?

Friend: An ally that is indeed of substance.

Director: But the fluff still seems to be inconsequential to evil.

Friend: Yes, and that's to its advantage.

Director: Because the fluff is spying on evil.

Friend: Yes.

Director: And there are certain dangers associated with spying, no?

Friend: This is true. But the fluff is happy to take the risk.

Director: Why?

6

Friend: The fluff is willing to run the risk of giving knowledge of evil to the good because out of this arrangement he derives a feeling of worth.

Director: Can the fluff become good, itself, in the process?

Friend: Of course not.

Director: Why not?

Friend: It doesn't have the necessary nature.

Director: What is that nature?

Friend: It is one of virtue.

Director: Fluff has no virtue?

Friend: What virtue does it take to float around watching and listening to things?

Director: But wait. If a fluff reports to the good about the activities of evil, doesn't it have to be truthful in how it reports?

Friend: Yes, I suppose it does.

Director: Isn't truthfulness a virtue?

Friend: It is.

Director: Doesn't that make fluff like the good? Don't the good have truthful natures?

Friend: Yes, you have a point.

7

Director: Does fluff have any vices?

Friend: None that I can think of.

Director: So fluff has nothing in common with evil?

Friend: No, nothing.

Director: I suppose that's another reason why fluff seems inconsequential to evil.

Friend: Yes, and fluff's truthfulness is another reason why it seems consequential to good.

Director: But what if fluff wants to seem consequential to evil?

Friend: Why would it?

Director: Maybe it's taken with the idea of seeming consequential. Maybe after having been nothing but fluff for so long it longs to seem to be — nay, to be — of substance, to as many people as possible.

Friend: I don't know, Director. How would it do that and still be an ally to the good?

Director: It could lie to evil about good.

Friend: That sounds like a dangerous business.

Director: Is that the only objection you have?

Friend: That and the fact that the fluff would be ruining its character.

Director: Because of the lying.

Friend: Yes.

8

Director: What if the fluff doesn't lie to evil? What if the fluff tells the truth?

Friend: Then the fluff is a spy for both sides?

Director: Maybe "spy" is not the right word here. Maybe "ambassador" is?

Friend: Ambassador? Good would maintain good relations with evil by sending fluff?

Director: Yes.

Friend: Why on earth would the good do that?

Director: For the same reason the evil would — in order to build understanding.

Friend: Ha! Good and evil don't want to understand one another.

Director: Then maybe our friend the fluff takes matters into its own hands and travels between the two independently, carried on currents of air as they happen to flow, and shares the information it happens to have about the other side.

Friend: In hopes of building understanding.

Director: Yes.

Friend: That's crazy. Even if good and evil come to understand one another perfectly, despite themselves, they are still going to be evil and good. So I would say that if our fluff shares, it should do so with no hopes of building understanding — because it's pointless to think understanding will amount to anything here.

Director: Would our fluff be better off sharing only with the other fluffs it happens to meet?

Friend: Well, that would make it consequential to those like itself. And what more can someone ask than that? But if a fluff does ask for more, then he should resign himself to sharing only with the good.

DWELL

Persons of the Dialogue

Director

Friend

1

Director: You can't dwell on it.

Friend: But what if I made a mistake?

Director: What if you did?

Friend: I'd need to do something about it.

Director: But you're not sure you made a mistake.

Friend: True.

Director: What would it take to figure out if you did indeed make a mistake?

Friend: I'd have to reopen the matter.

Director: And reopen it with everyone who was involved?

Friend: Yes, as I said.

Director: What if those people would rather not have the matter reopened?

Friend: Why wouldn't they?

Director: Let's say they might find it tiresome.

Friend: But if I did indeed make a mistake involving them, how can I make amends if I don't get them involved?

Director: You can move on to what's next and this time do it to your satisfaction.

Friend: What about their satisfaction?

2

Director: They can always choose to ignore you, or even break off relations, if they don't like your work.

Friend: But that's so sad.

Director: It would be sadder still if you try only to please them. You need to please yourself.

Friend: But isn't that selfish?

Director: Yes, I suppose it is. But do you think it's harmful, or destructive, selfishness?

Friend: No, I guess it's not. But how do I not dwell on what's been done?

Director: You get to work with all your heart on the next thing.

Friend: Work is my salvation.

Director: Indeed.

Friend: But what if I keep on making mistakes?

Director: You'll have to learn from them.

Friend: People always say that. But I'm not sure they know how painful it is to learn something that way, to really learn it.

Director: Not all learning is painful, is it?

Friend: Well, maybe not. But this sort of learning certainly is.

3

Director: But what are you going to learn? You're not planning to make mistakes, are you?

Friend: No. I just need to learn how not to dwell on what might have been a mistake.

Director: But it might not — to repeat, not — have been a mistake at all, right?

Friend: That's right. When I finished, things seemed quite good to me.

Director: And it was only when you got feedback that you started to doubt.

Friend: That means I don't believe in myself enough, doesn't it?

Director: Maybe that belief is what you need in order to move on.

Friend: Yes, I think you're right.

Director: What happens if you move on without belief in yourself?

Friend: You feel like you're hollow.

Director: Are you more likely to make mistakes if you feel hollow, or if you feel solid?

Friend: Hollow, without doubt.

Director: And, to be sure, how do you feel solid?

Friend: You believe in yourself. There's no other way.

Director: If you believe in yourself, can you live with not knowing whether something you did was a mistake or not?

Friend: I think you can, but it will be hard. It might haunt you.

4

Director: But if you believe in yourself and focus on your work, shouldn't things get better with time?

Friend: I think they should.

Director: Then you know what to do.

Friend: Knowing is one thing. Doing is another.

Director: Well, let me ask you this. What are you more likely to dwell on — something you know was a mistake, or something you're not sure was a mistake?

Friend: Something you're not sure about.

Director: Remind me of why we don't simply reopen things in order to determine whether such a thing was a mistake or not.

Friend: Well, in my case, I could reopen things on my own. But I don't think that's enough. I'd need the others who were involved to get involved again. You said they might find that tiresome.

Director: Why do you think they might find it tiresome, if that's the right word?

Friend: Because the mistake I made was bad.

Director: Did any of them tell you that you made a mistake, let alone a bad mistake?

Friend: Well, no.

Director: Didn't some of them even encourage you?

Friend: Yes, but I think they were just trying to be nice.

5

Director: Regardless, why do you think they might not want to get back into it?

Friend: I don't know. Why?

Director: Maybe it wasn't a big deal to them.

Friend: Or maybe it was a very big deal.

Director: True, that is possible.

Friend: But let's focus on what you said. What seems huge to me may seem small to them.

Director: Yes. That's how it often is, you know. Now, what's the only way to make things like this seem less than huge?

Friend: Perspective.

Director: How do you gain perspective?

Friend: You move on.

Director: And what do you do in order to move on?

Friend: You get back to work.

Director: So you stop dwelling on what may have been a mistake, and start dwelling on... what?

Friend: The present, and what can be done now.

Director: What can be done now?

Friend: Good work that shows learning from what may or may not have been mistakes in the past.

6

Director: Can you learn more from mistakes, or from what may or may not have been mistakes?

Friend: I think you can learn more from what may or may not have been mistakes.

Director: Why?

Friend: With things that you know are mistakes, you know exactly what's involved — why they were mistakes. But with things that may or may not have been mistakes, there are many more factors. You have to examine all of them.

Director: So with a mistake, there may be ten things involved. But with something that may or may not have been a mistake, there may be a hundred things involved?

Friend: Maybe even a thousand.

Director: What's the difference between examining and dwelling?

Friend: Examining is active. Dwelling can be passive.

Director: Like ruminating?

Friend: Yes, exactly.

Director: Tell me when you ruminate.

Friend: You ruminate when you've already been over things many, many times. You keep on going while introducing nothing new into the process. You just go over things again and again and again.

Director: But don't you have to do that when you are examining things?

Friend: Maybe when examining you go over things a few times, to make sure you're not missing anything. But it's a different state of mind. Examination is incisive. Rumination is not.

7

Director: When you talked about dwelling in the now, were you thinking about either examining or ruminating?

Friend: I wasn't thinking of either of those.

Director: But would you ruminate on what you are working on?

Friend: No, I think that's a bad idea.

Director: Because rumination is simply bad?

Friend: I don't know that I'd say it's simply bad.

Director: When is it good?

Friend: I guess it's good when something requires long and slow attention.

Director: Like a seemingly insoluble problem?

Friend: Yes, exactly.

Director: A problem like whether you made a mistake or not?

Friend: What are you trying to say? I thought we agreed I need to move on.

Director: Maybe you can do both — move on, yet continue to chew on the problem of what may or may not have been a mistake.

Friend: But isn't that a recipe for self-torture?

Director: Not if you work and chew at the same time. It might even be soothing.

Friend: I could use some soothing. Do you think I'll ever find the answer as to whether it was a mistake or not?

Director: Maybe you will. And maybe you won't. But that's no longer the point now, is it?

Friend: No, I guess it isn't. The point is that I now have something to help me in my work. Doubt is the price of creativity.

Persons of the Dialogue

Director

Friend

1

Friend: But what if I reveal too much?

Director: What does it mean to reveal too much?

Friend: To tell more than you ought to.

Director: Why shouldn't you tell more than you "ought to"?

Friend: Because what you say can be used against you.

Director: What do you have to say that can be used against you?

Friend: Oh, anything — personal details that you don't want everyone to know.

Director: Why don't you want everyone to know about them?

Friend: Because they are embarrassing.

Director: That's it?

Friend: You say that as if you wouldn't mind if things about you were revealed.

Director: I just meant to question whether anything else but embarrassment happens.

Friend: Well, certain things follow from embarrassment.

Director: You mean like a loss of face?

Friend: Exactly.

Director: What is face good for?

Friend: Your standing with your peers.

2

Director: So what you reveal can affect your standing.

Friend: Now do you see why it's so important?

Director: Is that really all that's at stake?

Friend: Again, you make it sound like it's nothing to be concerned about.

Director: I just want to know if you are afraid, in addition, that you'll become the object of ridicule.

Friend: I admit it — I'm especially afraid of that.

Director: What's wrong with being ridiculed, aside from losing face?

Friend: Are you serious? It hurts, Director — it hurts.

Director: Does it hurt no matter what has been revealed?

Friend: What do you mean?

Director: I mean, what if what is revealed is nothing wrong?

Friend: You mean it is simply embarrassing and nothing else?

Director: Yes.

Friend: Well, I suppose that's better than having revealed something that you did that was wrong.

Director: Have you done things that are wrong?

Friend: Well, sort of — yes.

3

Director: And you have done things that are embarrassing — beyond mere "personal details"?

Friend: I definitely have.

Director: You've never revealed anything of either sort to me.

Friend: I've never revealed anything of either sort to anyone.

Director: Why not?

Friend: Because I'm afraid of what will happen if word gets out.

Director: You don't trust that the person will keep your confidence?

Friend: That's right.

Director: Do you feel you have a burden that you carry in these secrets?

Friend: Yes.

Director: Would it make you feel better to share the wrong and embarrassing things?

Friend: I don't know.

Director: But you're not willing to find out?

Friend: No, I'm not. But what about you, Director. Have you done things that were embarrassing?

Director: Embarrassing to me or to someone else?

Friend: To you, Director — to you.

Director: I'm not sure.

4

Friend: How can you not be sure?

Director: What is embarrassing?

Friend: Things you don't want others to know about.

Director: But then the embarrassing would include the wrong, at least from what we've been saying.

Friend: Okay, fair enough. The embarrassing is that which makes you blush. When's the last time you blushed?

Director: I'd rather not say.

Friend: Why, because you've never blushed?

Director: I blushed, once.

Friend: Why did you blush?

Director: Because I was embarrassed.

Friend: Why were you embarrassed?

Director: Because I was wrong about something that I felt sure about.

Friend: What was it?

Director: I realized that what I was doing was not right.

Friend: Ah, you have done something wrong!

Director: Try not to sound so triumphant.

5

Friend: Can you blame me? What was it?

Director: I can trust you?

Friend: Of course!

Director: You won't tell anyone?

Friend: No, no — certainly not.

Director: I was contradicting anyone and everyone who seemed to me to be mistaken about anything at all.

Friend: But you do that now.

Director: Not to the degree I once did.

Friend: Why did you conclude this wasn't right?

Director: Because it wasn't helpful.

Friend: You had to learn to choose your battles?

Director: Yes. And do you know why?

Friend: Why?

Director: I was revealing too much about myself in the process of contradicting.

Friend: Ha! You were losing face?

Director: So to speak.

Friend: And this embarrassed you?

Director: No, it made me think.

6

Friend: What did you think?

Director: That I had been going about things the wrong way.

Friend: And that embarrassed you.

Director: Yes.

Friend: Why?

Director: Because I was so sure it was the right way.

Friend: Who saw you blush?

Director: No one.

Friend: You blushed when you were all alone?

Director: Yes.

Friend: I didn't think that was possible. So how do you go about things now?

Director: I'm careful about who I reveal myself to.

Friend: By "reveal" you mean argue with?

Director: Or have a discussion with — yes.

Friend: Are you having better results?

Director: Yes, much.

Friend: So I take it you never argue or discuss things with strangers.

7

Director: Oh, no. Sometimes strangers are the best people to talk to.

Friend: Why?

Director: They can have interesting perspectives.

Friend: And you just feel free to reveal to them everything about you?

Director: Not everything. But I sometimes tell them about my wrong and my embarrassment.

Friend: And here I was thinking I was your special confidant. You don't really have special confidants, do you?

Director: But I do. You're the one who doesn't.

Friend: True enough, about me.

Director: Friend, I don't just tell anyone about my wrong and my embarrassment.

Friend: Perfect strangers don't count as "anyone"?

Director: It depends on the stranger. Each stranger is different, don't you think?

Friend: Of course. So what do these strangers and I have in common?

Director: You listen without judging.

Friend: But a rock or a tree can listen without judging.

Director: You listen without judging negatively.

Friend: You're looking for a sympathetic ear.

Director: Yes, when it comes to revealing things.

8

Friend: You think I should reveal things to sympathetic ears?

Director: That's up to you, Friend. I'm not trying to persuade you to do so with me.

Friend: Why not? Don't you want to know?

Director: There are many things I want to know. Your private business isn't among them.

Friend: But what if I want to share with you? Would you listen?

Director: I would listen to a point.

Friend: To what point?

Director: To the point where I think you might regret what you reveal.

Friend: Why would I regret?

Director: Because you might become uncomfortable with me later, especially if others are around.

Friend: Because with the others I would act as though I didn't have things I didn't want them to know about — and there you would be, knowing.

Director: Yes. Some might find that to be disconcerting.

Friend: But what about what I know about you? Won't you find that disconcerting?

Director: What, that I used to contradict everyone all the time?

Friend: I take your point. You don't really have anything to be ashamed of, do you?

Director: And you do?

9

Friend: I most certainly do.

Director: Things that you did that were wrong?

Friend: Yes.

Director: Then I'm sorry, Friend.

Friend: Don't be sorry. It's my own fault.

Director: I don't like to see you with a heavy heart.

Friend: What can I do? I have things I must carry within me. Or do you think I should ease my burden with a stranger?

Director: Would you like me to arrange a meeting?

Friend: What? You're serious?

Director: Yes. You can speak with someone you'll most likely never see again, someone who'll listen sympathetically.

Friend: How do you know he'll be sympathetic?

Director: Because I know you, and I know him.

Friend: You already have someone in mind?

Director: I do. He's here until tomorrow night when he flies back home.

Friend: Ha! Oh, how tempting. Thank you. But I'm going to decline.

Director: Why?

10

Friend: How do I know he's not going to tell you, or somehow tell someone who tells someone who knows me?

Director: I trust him to be discreet.

Friend: I'm the one who needs to have that trust.

Director: Why don't we get together with him tonight, and then, if you see fit, you can meet with him alone tomorrow. His day is free.

Friend: I'm interviewing a priest to see if I should confess to him?

Director: Call it whatever you like.

Friend: Do you think he will... will... forgive me?

Director: I think the chance of that is very good. He is a man of broad and deep experience who understands many things. But you'll still have your burden to carry. He's not going to pretend to take away even some of it for you. And he may assign you penance, as it were, on top of it.

Friend: I'm prepared for that. Forgiveness would mean the world to me, you know.

Director: I know. Shall we go and meet him?

Friend: Does he know about me?

Director: I haven't said a word about you to him. I just told him that I might be bringing a friend.

Friend: I appreciate that, Director. Let's go and meet him.

Step Back

Persons of the Dialogue

Director

Friend

1

Director: You're too close to it.

Friend: What do you think I need to do?

Director: Step back.

Friend: You mean disengage?

Director: Yes.

Friend: But isn't that to admit defeat?

Director: I thought you weren't engaged in a contest.

Friend: Strictly speaking, I'm not.

Director: Let's speak strictly. I think you need some time to digest your experience.

Friend: And then I'll come back all the stronger?

Director: Maybe.

Friend: Maybe?

Director: Maybe you won't want to come back.

Friend: But then I'm a quitter.

Director: Some things warrant quitting.

Friend: How will I know when I should consider quitting?

Director: You'll feel it.

2

Friend: Feel it? So if I feel bad about something I should think about quitting, and if I feel good about something I should stick it out? What about things that start out feeling bad but feel good once you get the hang of them?

Director: I wasn't saying you'll feel good or bad about the thing.

Friend: What were you saying?

Director: You'll feel you have no choice but to stay with it.

Friend: And that's exactly when I should step back, and then decide whether or not to quit?

Director: Yes.

Friend: But then you're saying that I should stick it out when I feel I do have a choice?

Director: Yes, if you want to — if you choose. How do you feel about what you're doing now?

Friend: Like I have no choice but to keep at it.

Director: So you're going to step back, right?

Friend: I guess so. And if I come to feel like I have a choice again, I can go back?

Director: Yes.

Friend: So I should always feel like I have a choice.

Director: That's the idea.

Friend: But it's just an idea, isn't it? I mean, what if I really have no choice, not even to step back for a short while?

Director: You can always step back, even if you still have to go through the motions.

3

Friend: You're talking about stepping back mentally.

Director: Yes.

Friend: But can you do that if you don't have the motions down?

Director: You mean like when you're starting something new?

Friend: Yes. What if you're still learning the motions? Don't you have to step forward fully for that?

Director: Not necessarily.

Friend: Then how are you going to learn?

Director: Part of you can learn the motions while the other part, the stepped back part, can digest the experience.

Friend: And that's what stepping back is all about — digestion?

Director: Yes, for the hard to digest things. It's the best way to prevent or cure mental indigestion.

Friend: You mean from taking in too much, or taking in the wrong things?

Director: Yes.

Friend: Why not eat, or learn, first, fully stepped forward, and digest later?

Director: Don't you know that proper digestion begins right away, with the teeth?

Friend: Yes, but how many people, outside of our digestion metaphor, step back to reflect as soon as the learning without choice begins?

Director: Certainly not all of them. And that's one of the reasons why we've got a number of sick people in this world.

4

Friend: So you are saying there is no real choice but to step back at once, when you feel you have no choice about something, and try to digest the experience?

Director: Well, you can always continue to gorge without digesting, and then purge.

Friend: That's no choice. So what part of your mind steps back?

Director: Have you ever heard someone say that he is making a mental reservation?

Friend: Yes.

Director: That part.

Friend: You make reservations about what you are learning?

Director: You do.

Friend: And what do you do with those reservations?

Director: You see if you can digest them or not.

Friend: And if you can't?

Director: You may need to step back more than mentally.

Friend: But what if you can't do that? I mean, what if what you have a problem with is simply the way things are, wherever you go?

Director: You mean you have no choice? Then you need to change the way things are.

5

Friend: Ha! How is one person supposed to do that?

Director: The same way other people in the past have done exactly that.

Friend: How?

Director: One difficult step at a time.

Friend: So the first such step is the stepping back.

Director: Yes.

Friend: What's the next step? Or is that precisely what you can't tell me?

Director: You understand very well.

Friend: Understanding is one thing. Doing is another.

Director: Doing brings its own understanding, its own knowing, Friend.

Friend: So I should just step blindly until I understand, until I know?

Director: No, I recommend you keep your eyes open.

Friend: No — I mean, you're saying I should simply do, do without understanding, do without knowing what will happen.

Director: If you understood, if you knew, exactly what would happen every time you did something, wouldn't that be boring?

Friend: Many people would prefer boring, you know.

Director: Is that what you prefer?

Friend: No, I guess it's not.

6

Director: If you're doing things that are not boring, that are interesting, would you want to stay stepped forward, by your own choice?

Friend: I suppose I would.

Director: And you would know you could always step back, at least mentally, if necessary, in order to digest something difficult.

Friend: Yes.

Director: So why not do something interesting?

Friend: You make it sound like it's so easy to find something interesting to do.

Director: Isn't it?

Friend: No.

Director: Why not? I mean, don't you know what you are interested in?

Friend: That's half the problem.

Director: You don't know?

Friend: I don't.

Director: So you just try things randomly in hopes you'll find something you are interested in?

Friend: That's pretty much how I've gone about it.

Director: Do you think that's foolish, Friend?

Friend: I don't see how I have any other choice.

7

Director: It's good that you'll be stepping back from what you're doing now.

Friend: I agree. Can you help me find something interesting?

Director: Not until you find what interests you.

Friend: How can I do that? Nothing jumps out to me as interesting.

Director: What do you like to do?

Friend: I like to have conversations with you.

Director: That's a start. What about our conversations do you like?

Friend: You challenge me.

Director: Where can you find challenging conversations?

Friend: I don't want any old challenging conversation.

Director: Why not?

Friend: Because many challengers are too aggressive. Many challengers lack understanding.

Director: My challenges aren't aggressive? My challenges don't lack understanding?

Friend: No. Your challenges are gentle. And you show understanding.

Director: So where can you find gentle, understanding challenges?

Friend: I don't know.

8

Director: What if you challenge yourself?

Friend: I don't know how to do that.

Director: Oh, it's easy. I do it to myself all the time.

Friend: How do I get started?

Director: You can pretend I'm there with you, wherever you might be, and you can play both my part and your part in the conversation. Then, when you've gotten good at this, you can drop me altogether and just have conversations with yourself. Just make sure you remember to be gentle and understanding. It's easy to forget.

Friend: So I can do this when I step back from a situation.

Director: Yes. And such internal dialogue can help you digest your experience thoroughly.

Friend: But to start out, can we have real conversations during my stepping back?

Director: Yes, of course. In fact, let's consider this the first conversation of your stepping back.

Friend: Yes, let's. You know, I think it helped.

Director: Good. Let's see where it, and others like it, lead.

Not My Thing

Persons of the Dialogue

Director

Friend

1

Friend: He embarrassed me terribly.

Director: How? What happened?

Friend: He recommended a philosophy book very highly. So I went out and bought it and started to read it. But I just couldn't get into it. So I set it aside. The next time I saw him he asked me, in front of all our friends, what I thought about the book. I told him it wasn't my thing.

Director: Then what happened?

Friend: He asked me to be specific about what I didn't like. I told him that nothing resonated with me, that I didn't enjoy it.

Director: And?

Friend: He said that it's a book you have to work at. I told him I'm not looking for a book like that now. But then he asked me if I knew what the book was about.

Director: What's it about?

Friend: Well, philosophy. I told him so. He asked if I knew what philosophy is about.

Director: What did you tell him?

Friend: Wisdom.

Director: What happened then?

Friend: Everyone laughed.

2

Director: Did he say what he thinks philosophy is about?

Friend: Yes — thinking. And then do you know what he did? He said that since a book about thinking didn't resonate with me, I must not be very good at thinking. And they laughed some more.

Director: That was rotten of them. I'm sorry you had that run in, Friend.

Friend: Thanks — me, too. But do you know what the worst part is?

Director: What?

Friend: That I believe they're right — that philosophy is about thinking, and I'm not good at it.

Director: You think you're not good at thinking because a particular book doesn't resonate with you?

Friend: It's a very influential book.

Director: So what? If it's not your thing, it's not your thing. Right?

Friend: I guess so.

Director: These guys really have you down, don't they?

Friend: Yes. They make me want to take the book back up again.

Director: Do you want to be like them?

Friend: No, of course not.

Director: Then why do you want to share things with them, like this book?

Friend: Because I'm afraid I'm not a very good thinker.

Director: And if you can master this book you can show yourself that you are?

Friend: Yes.

3

Director: It's important to you to know that you are a good thinker.

Friend: It is.

Director: Why?

Friend: Because... well... thinking is the most important thing we do.

Director: How do you know that?

Friend: Doesn't everyone know that?

Director: People who don't think very much most likely don't.

Friend: Yes, but what if they don't think much, but when they do, they think well?

Director: When do you think we need to think?

Friend: When we're trying to figure something out.

Director: And it's important to figure things out?

Friend: Yes, of course.

Director: Why?

Friend: So you can do what you want to do.

Director: This book you bought, if you figure it out, what will you be able to do?

Friend: I guess I'd be able to show those rotten friends of mine that I can think, too.

Director: Is that a good reason to figure the book out?

Friend: Well, maybe not.

4

Director: I wonder if that's why the book doesn't resonate with you.

Friend: Why?

Director: Because you don't have a good reason to read it.

Friend: You think if I had a good reason it might?

Director: Yes.

Friend: And you're not talking about having to read it for school, are you?

Director: No.

Friend: What do you think is a good reason to read a book?

Director: You'd know if you had one. How? The book would speak to you, really speak to you.

Friend: But what if you have to read the book many times before it starts to speak to you, before it starts to resonate?

Director: Well, if you have reason to believe that's the case, because of some initial spark, then, sure, keep reading to see if it really lights up. But without that spark, I wouldn't bother with it. Life's too short.

Friend: Isn't it like that with other things than books?

Director: Yes.

Friend: So if what someone says doesn't resonate with you, you won't continue to speak with him for long?

Director: That's right.

5

Friend: You think when you talk to people, don't you?

Director: Yes.

Friend: And that thinking is no different than the thinking you do when you read?

Director: I think it's fair to say that thinking is thinking.

Friend: So if I am thinking when I talk to people, I don't need a book to prove I can think.

Director: That sounds right to me.

Friend: Do you agree that thinking is the most important thing that we do?

Director: Let's say that thinking is a tool. A tool is only as important as the use to which it's put. To what end would you put your thinking?

Friend: To the end of wisdom.

Director: And to what end do your rotten friends put their thinking?

Friend: They talk about achieving clarity and understanding.

Director: There doesn't seem to be anything wrong with that.

Friend: True, but they see clarity and understanding as ends themselves.

Director: Don't you see wisdom that way?

Friend: No, I don't.

Director: Can you say more?

6

Friend: Wisdom is about what you do. Wisdom gets you what you want. It serves other ends than itself. You can be clear about and understand something all you want, but without wisdom you'll never obtain it.

Director: Can you act from wisdom without clarity and understanding?

Friend: That's a good question. No, I suppose you can't — or rather, why would you? I mean, if you're not clear about the thing you want, and if you don't understand it, what point is there to getting it?

Director: So where does that leave us?

Friend: We need to think in order to obtain clarity and understanding, and in order to gain wisdom.

Director: Do you need that book to think your way to clarity and understanding?

Friend: No — not as long as I have someone like you to talk to.

Director: And what about wisdom? Do you need the book to think your way to that?

Friend: No, I don't.

Director: Tell me, Friend — have we been thinking just now?

Friend: Yes — and thinking well.

Director: What is the fruit of this thought? What are you clear about, what do you understand — and what will you do?

Friend: It's clear to me, and I understand, that that book is not important to me. I will leave it alone and pay no attention to those rotten friends of mine. In fact, I don't think we'll be friends any longer at all. Thanks for going through this with me, Director. I'm feeling much better now.

KNOWING

1

Friend: Sometimes it's harder to know than not to know.

Director: When is it harder?

Friend: When it involves something that isn't easy to come to terms with.

Director: What does that mean, to come to terms with?

Friend: To accept.

Director: What if you don't accept?

Friend: Then you'll never know.

Director: And that, too, can be hard.

Friend Yes.

Director: What about the wise man who knows many things? Is it easy for him?

Friend: You don't get wise by easy experience.

Director: But what about in the end, when you've wrung your knowledge from the experiences you've had — is it easier?

Friend: I don't know. But what about for you, Director? Do you have it easy?

Director: What do you think I know?

Friend: I think you know many things about people.

Director: You mean like who does what?

Friend: No, I mean about people in general.

2

Director: You think I know how people tend to be, what they are?

Friend: Yes, exactly. Does that knowledge sit easily with you?

Director: I don't know that I know much about people in general. I believe my knowledge is limited to people I actually know. But you know many people, many individuals, don't you, Friend?

Friend: Yes.

Director: Do you like what you know about some of them?

Friend: No, I don't.

Director: Does that knowledge sit easily with you?

Friend: It doesn't.

Director: Well then, you can imagine how it is for me.

Friend: But is there no end to the difficulty?

Director: Do you find it difficult to talk to me?

Friend: Not at all.

Director: Then maybe friendship is what can ease the burden of difficult knowledge.

Friend: Are you saying that, as you gain in such knowledge, you must also gain in friends?

Director: New friends can help. But you don't necessarily have to have them. The friends you have now might suit you just fine as your knowledge grows.

3

Friend: And in order for your knowledge to grow concerning difficult things you must have more difficult experiences.

Director: Would you prefer not to have the knowledge?

Friend: That's precisely what I'm wondering.

Director: Well, don't worry, Friend. It's not entirely up to you.

Friend: What do you mean?

Director: Experiences will happen to you whether you want them to or not.

Friend: So the only choice is in how you deal with them.

Director: That's right.

Friend: And how should you deal with them?

Director: Learn what you can.

Friend: But how?

Director: Come to terms with your experiences.

Friend: I thought that's what you might say.

Director: Do you think it's bad advice?

Friend: No, but I think it's advice that is sometimes hard to take.

Director: But why? Would you rather not come to terms with your experiences?

Friend: What do you think that would be like?

4

Director: Not coming to terms with your experiences is like eating without digesting, to the point where you become painfully sick — spiritually.

Friend: That doesn't sound very good. So you simply have to accept your experiences.

Director: Yes.

Friend: Then what do you do in order to gain knowledge from them?

Director: Think about them.

Friend: Yes, but what does it mean to think about things like this?

Director: First of all, dwelling is not thinking. Thinking is active. But allow your thoughts to develop over a period of time. Don't rush them. And try not to force them from your consciousness when they appear.

Friend: I've done that, the forcing.

Director: How did it go?

Friend: It only made things worse.

Director: Then I suggest that you allow your consciousness to gently integrate the experiences you've had into your personal history, into part of who you are.

Friend: That's what I'm afraid of, you know.

Director: Having your experiences as a part of you?

Friend: Yes. Why do your experiences have to be a part of you at all, of who you really are?

5

Director: Are you thinking it's unfair because you can't always choose your experiences?

Friend: Exactly. Why can't I be what I choose to be? Isn't that what it means to be an individual?

Director: A true individual knows he can't always be what he would like to be. He has to be what he is. But experiences can be overcome.

Friend: Is the way to do that through knowledge?

Director: Yes.

Friend: So if you really integrate your experiences into your history, into part of who you are, is that where you can start to gain knowledge?

Director: Yes, and not a minute before.

Friend: Why not?

Director: Because you can't see your experiences clearly until you've truly made them your own.

Friend: So when you see your experiences clearly, what do you do?

Director: Try to know what they mean.

Friend: Mean about you?

Director: Yes, but also the world — your world.

Friend: Your world? Are you saying your experiences aren't universal?

Director: Do you think they are?

Friend: I'm not sure.

6

Director: Well, we each live within a world that touches on other worlds, some worlds more than others.

Friend: And that's as much as we can know?

Director: That's how it seems to me.

Friend: But what if some people share certain experiences? What if they share a world?

Director: I don't think that changes things as far as universals go.

Friend: Not even if everyone has the same experiences, at least some of the more basic kinds?

Director: Why do you want for these universals to exist?

Friend: Because then the knowledge gained from them would be universally applicable.

Director: You're wondering how you can apply your knowledge?

Friend: Yes. I mean, so what if I gain knowledge that only applies to my own private experiences, my own world?

Director: So what? Won't you learn how to act better within your own world, and how to act better as you touch other worlds?

Friend: I guess.

Director: Think of what you'll have in common with the people in these other worlds — not universals, but good interactions.

Friend: And that's what it's all about? Good interactions?

Director: Don't you think it should be? After all, we're interacting until the day we die.

7

Friend: So it's never too late to learn.

Director: No, never.

Friend: That's encouraging.

Director: I'm glad you think so.

Friend: But I have a question, Director. What about these people who urge you to go out and have all sorts of interactions, all sorts of experiences?

Director: What do you mean?

Friend: Aren't they foolish? Experience will happen whatever you do, so why seek it out?

Director: It depends on your world.

Friend: How?

Director: You might have a small world, one that could use an increase in size.

Friend: But how would you know how small is too small?

Director: You'll feel crowded in it.

Friend: So the search for more room results in experiences.

Director: Yes, naturally.

Friend: But once your world has expanded, can you ever go back to something smaller?

Director: I'm afraid not.

8

Friend: What happens if you try to go back?

Director: Guess.

Friend: You feel terribly crowded, more than before — and worse.

Director: Exactly.

Friend: So where does that leave us?

Director: I think we agree that knowledge is good, if very difficult at times. What do you think?

Friend: I think that's true. But more importantly, the knowledge you gain from bad experiences allows you to rise above those experiences. Can we say more about this?

Director: What would you like to say?

Friend: Is overcoming really as simple as gaining knowledge?

Director: Not quite. You also have to live up to the knowledge you gain. And that's another discussion for another time.

WORRY

Persons of the Dialogue

Director

Friend

1

Director: What is it, Friend?

Friend: Oh, nothing. I just can't stop worrying.

Director: You know what they say is the tried and true measure to counter worry, don't you?

Friend: Yes, work.

Director: Have you tried it?

Friend: Have I tried it? That's all I do! I work, and work, and work, until I pass out from exhaustion at night.

Director: Does it help?

Friend: Yes.

Director: Why do you think you worry?

Friend: Because I care.

Director: Would it be possible to care and not worry?

Friend: I don't see how.

Director: But isn't it more or less universally agreed that worry does no good?

Friend: It is. But I don't believe it.

Director: You believe your worry does good?

Friend: Yes.

Director: How?

2

Friend: If something bad happens, and I haven't been worrying about it, I will never be able to forgive myself.

Director: Is that because worry is all you can do about some things, things that are out of your control, and if you're not worrying, you've been somehow negligent?

Friend: Precisely.

Director: And on the flip side, are you hoping that your worry will somehow bring a sort of cosmic justice to protect what you care about, be they people or things?

Friend: Yes.

Director: But you know, don't you, that harm has, in the past, come to people and things that have been worried over?

Friend: Maybe it wasn't the right kind of worry.

Director: I see. And do you know that there have been people and things that had no one worrying over them that have come through unscathed?

Friend: Maybe someone unknown was worrying about them.

Director: But you must know on some level that worry really does no good.

Friend: I don't know that, Director.

Director: Have you ever experienced what it's like not to worry?

Friend: I haven't. Except....

Director: Except?

3

Friend: Except for these moments when I suddenly realize that I'm not worrying. And I feel during those moments that I could just go on not worrying. But you know what happens?

Director: What?

Friend: That worries me!

Director: So you go back to worrying.

Friend: Yes, right away.

Director: Perhaps there's a way to moderate your worrying.

Friend: How?

Director: Maybe for one hour you tell yourself that nothing bad will happen. Let that really settle in. And then the next hour allow yourself to worry that something bad might happen. Then start again.

Friend: Director, that will drive me crazy.

Director: More so than worrying constantly? This would amount to a fifty percent drop in worry.

Friend: I don't think I could take the back and forth.

Director: So then the choice is to worry all of the time, or worry none of the time?

Friend: Yes, and it's no choice for me.

Director: What would it take to get you to stop worrying?

Friend: To me, worry is just a part of life.

4

Director: Do you think worry is a way of life for everyone?

Friend: No, I don't.

Director: What do you think makes the difference?

Friend: I think some people just don't care as much as I do.

Director: Care about what?

Friend: Everything.

Director: Is your job, your work, a part of "everything"?

Friend: Yes.

Director: Does worry do it any good?

Friend: Yes, in fact.

Director: How?

Friend: It makes me extra conscientious.

Director: Do you think other people can be as conscientious but without the same amount of worry?

Friend: I don't know. Maybe.

Director: Maybe you need to believe in yourself more.

Friend: You think that would help with the worry?

Director: Yes.

5

Friend: What do I need in order to believe in myself?

Director: Courage.

Friend: Are you implying I don't have courage now?

Director: No. When you're worried about something, I would say it takes courage to go on and deal with it.

Friend: So I'm courageous despite my worry, provided I deal with it.

Director: Yes.

Friend: What do you think it takes to deal with it?

Director: Why don't you tell me what you think?

Friend: Dealing with it means using it as a source of strength.

Director: How so?

Friend: Things that seem difficult to others seem like nothing to me, when I compare them to my worry. I gladly take on the difficult since it takes my mind off of things.

Director: We may have gotten to the root of the problem.

Friend: What do you mean?

Director: You depend on your worry for strength.

Friend: Isn't it better to put it to some use than not?

Director: But you'll never get rid of your worry this way.

6

Friend: Why would I want to get rid of my worry if it gives me strength?

Director: Would you say that, all things being equal, strength either way, if you had the choice, you would rather worry than not?

Friend: Well, I don't know that all things can really be equal here.

Director: What if we found you a replacement source of strength?

Friend: Are you going to tell me that the replacement is belief in myself?

Director: What do you think? Could that work?

Friend: Well, if I believe in myself, I won't be afraid to take on the difficult. I will have confidence that I can do it. Right?

Director: That's the idea. So which would you rather have? Strength from worry, or strength from confidence?

Friend: Strength from worry.

Director: But why?

Friend: I don't believe in myself enough.

Director: What do you think it would take in order to believe in yourself enough?

Friend: I don't know.

Director: When you take on difficult things out of worry, do you have success?

Friend: I do.

Director: More often than not?

Friend: Yes.

7

Director: Well then, you're successful.

Friend: I am.

Director: Haven't you heard that success breeds confidence?

Friend: I have.

Director: Do you believe it's true?

Friend: Not in my case.

Director: Why not?

Friend: I don't believe that I can repeat the success.

Director: Why?

Friend: I believe that it depended on luck.

Director: Luck? You think it's possible to get lucky more often than not?

Friend: Yes.

Director: So you're a lucky guy.

Friend: That's how it seems to me.

Director: Then why not believe in your luck?

Friend: Because then I'll worry that I'm being over-confident.

Director: Tell me, Friend. Do you think that to be confident is really to be over-confident?

Friend: It's funny you should ask. Yes, I do. There's so much that can go wrong that confidence is actually over-confidence.

8

Director: But you can deal with what goes wrong, right?

Friend: True.

Director: Have you dealt with things that have gone wrong in the past?

Friend: I have.

Director: Did they turn out okay?

Friend: Mostly, yes.

Director: So you're mostly successful at dealing with things that go wrong.

Friend: I am.

Director: It seems you have every reason to be confident, except for this fear that to be confident is really to be over-confident. This may be the true root of your worry.

Friend: I think you're right.

Director: Why can't you let go and just be confident?

Friend: Because I'm afraid.

Director: Afraid of what?

Friend: Everything. I really am I coward, I suppose.

Director: You're afraid everything will go wrong?

Friend: Yes.

9

Director: You're going to have to stop thinking that way.

Friend: But I can't.

Director: Yes you can.

Friend: How?

Director: I will help you.

Friend: But what can you do?

Director: Show you that not everything goes wrong.

Friend: What if that's not enough?

Director: You're worried about our anti-worry strategy?

Friend: I am.

Director: Well, just leave that to me. There, that can be your first assignment.

Friend: You're going to give me anti-worry assignments?

Director: Yes. We'll get you in shape, one way or another.

Friend: Thanks for working with me on this, Director.

Director: No problem. I have an interest in getting to the point where I can stop my worrying, too — my worry about you!

LIGHT

Persons of the Dialogue

Director

Friend

1

Friend: Why does philosophy always have to be so heavy?

Director: It doesn't.

Friend: How can you make it light?

Director: You can write it as prose instead of poetry.

Friend: Who writes philosophy in poetry?

Director: Oh, many philosophers.

Friend: But philosophers generally write in prose.

Director: Yes, but their prose is poetic.

Friend: Now I think you're playing with me. What do you think poetry is?

Director: Something that is highly concentrated. Something that takes a good deal of pondering for its meaning to come clear.

Friend: I have to admit, that describes an awful lot of philosophy. Why do philosophers not want their meaning to come clear right away?

Director: Oh, I think they do want it to come clear right away.

Friend: Then why do they write the way they do?

Director: They're trying to say a lot in a little bit of space.

Friend: So you're saying that to make things lighter you just water everything down to some degree.

Director: Yes.

2

Friend: Is that what you do when you write?

Director: Sometimes I concentrate things. Sometimes I dilute them.

Friend: Which do you do when?

Director: It depends on how much I have to say about a certain topic, on how I feel.

Friend: Have you written about the same topic in different ways?

Director: I have.

Friend: Which do you tend to like better?

Director: Oh, they're just different. There's no comparing.

Friend: Is it easier for you to write light things?

Director: Believe it or not, sometimes it's harder.

Friend: How can that be?

Director: When you have a lot to say, it takes some restraint to say little.

Friend: Your light things say little?

Director: Only by comparison to my heavy things.

Friend: But how do you know that? I mean, what if your light things say as much as your heavy things, but in a different way?

Director: I can tell by the way people react.

Friend: What do they say?

3

Director: They tell me that there's more in the heavy stuff than in the light.

Friend: How do they know that's the case?

Director: I suppose it's because they find more in it.

Friend: Do you think they find everything that you put in it?

Director: I don't know.

Friend: But could you sit down with them and ask?

Director: Should I have a checklist to run through?

Friend: No. But you know what I mean, don't you?

Director: I think I do. Do you know what the funny thing is?

Friend: What?

Director: Sometimes they find things that I didn't know were in there.

Friend: But how can that be? You know what you wrote.

Director: Of course. But it's one thing to write something, and another thing entirely to know what it means to someone else.

Friend: Are you saying that meaning varies from person to person?

Director: Yes.

Friend: But why?

Director: Because we all bring different experiences to what's written.

4

Friend: Doesn't that frustrate you?

Director: To the contrary. I think it's wonderful.

Friend: How so?

Director: It creates a space for dialogue.

Friend: Dialogue about the work.

Director: Yes. If everyone understood the work exactly the way I do, what's there to say?

Friend: So you value different interpretations, for what they make possible.

Director: Yes.

Friend: I don't know if I could stand that as an author.

Director: Oh, it's not so bad.

Friend: So when someone tells you about your work, you're often surprised?

Director: Constantly.

Friend: And that doesn't bother you.

Director: No. In fact, it often makes me laugh.

Friend: Laugh?

Director: Yes, a good laugh, one of pleasure.

Friend: You're pleased to be misunderstood?

5

Director: Friend, once I write something it's out of my hands. It's a little bark out on the ocean, subject wind and wave. I'm just happy to catch sight of it from time to time through another's eyes.

Friend: And that's why you laugh? Because you're happy?

Director: Yes.

Friend: But what happens if your reader is not friendly toward your cause?

Director: Well, I regret that. But there's nothing I can do.

Friend: But doesn't it bother you if someone is very critical?

Director: If it's good criticism, then no, not at all. But if it's malicious criticism, well, that does tend to bother me, I must admit. But not for long.

Friend: How do you get over it?

Director: I go right back to writing again.

Friend: Heavy or light?

Director: It just depends, Friend.

Friend: On what?

Director: How I feel.

Friend: That's all there is to your decision?

Director: Would you rather I write contrary to how I feel?

Friend: Can you do that?

Director: Oh, yes. I have experimented a bit, you know.

6

Friend: How does it feel to write something heavy when you're in the mood for something light?

Director: It's a bit tedious.

Friend: Does the quality suffer?

Director: Not that I can tell.

Friend: How about the other way around?

Director: I can write light when feeling heavy, and the quality seems fine.

Friend: So since it doesn't seem to matter either way, you simply write the way you feel.

Director: Yes.

Friend: Do you think people should read the way they feel?

Director: You mean only read light things when in a light mood, or heavy things when in a heavy mood?

Friend: Yes. What do you think?

Director: They'd have to know ahead of time which one is which, right?

Friend: That's right.

Director: How could they know without reading the material first?

Friend: I think you can get a pretty good idea early on.

Director: So if you read a couple of pages and things seem light, you can assume the rest is light, and so on with heavy things?

Friend: Don't you think that's how it goes?

7

Director: But what if the author switches it up?

Friend: You mean he puts light things in predominantly heavy works, and heavy things in predominantly light works?

Director: Yes.

Friend: Well, I think that's fine. In fact, I think it's good to mix things up.

Director: Because it's not good to be too heavy or too light?

Friend: Right.

Director: Do you think an author should try to strike the perfect balance?

Friend: What do you mean?

Director: I mean, perhaps there should be exactly as much lightness as heaviness in each and every work, or maybe there should be one predominantly heavy work for each predominantly light work.

Friend: I'm intrigued by the notion of having as much lightness as heaviness in each and every work.

Director: What intrigues you?

Friend: You wouldn't know if the work is heavy or light.

Director: No, you wouldn't.

Friend: I don't know if people would like that.

Director: Why not?

8

Friend: They like to know what they are reading.

Director: Why not simply know that it's a blend?

Friend: "Blend" isn't definite enough for many.

Director: Does this go to more than a particular work?

Friend: What do you mean?

Director: I mean, do people want to know if I am a heavy or a light author, so they know what to expect from me?

Friend: Yes, they do.

Director: If I have to be one or the other, what should I be?

Friend: Be light.

Director: Why?

Friend: More people will try reading you.

Director: But can I work some heavy things into my lightness?

Friend: From time to time, yes. Just don't do so to the point where you confuse people. They don't like that.

Director: But some people might enjoy a more robust blend.

Friend: True. I know I would.

Director: Well, my friend, then I will write for them. I will write for you.

GRATITUDE

Persons of the Dialogue

Director

Friend

1

Friend: But they're ungrateful to you!

Director: I don't see it that way.

Friend: You helped them, and what do they do for you? Nothing.

Director: How do you think I helped them?

Friend: You helped them see things more clearly.

Director: I should be grateful to them in that case.

Friend: Why?

Director: Don't you think that the more people who see things clearly, the better off we all are?

Friend: Yes, I suppose I do.

Director: Then you should be grateful to them, too.

Friend: But that's ridiculous.

Director: Ridiculous, but true — unless you think we're not better off when people see things clearly.

Friend: But the point is that the ones you help are better off, too. For that they should be grateful.

Director: What if we call it a wash? They don't owe any gratitude to me, and I

---

don't owe any gratitude to them.

2

Friend: You don't want any gratitude?

Director: Not particularly, no.

Friend: Why not?

Director: Because I don't think I deserve it.

Friend: What's more important than seeing things clearly?

Director: Not much, if anything. But the point is that I didn't make them see things clearly. They came to see things on their own.

Friend: But you played a role — an important role.

Director: What did I do?

Friend: You showed them their errors.

Director: And how did I do that?

Friend: Through dialogue with them.

Director: What was the essence of this dialogue?

Friend: Persuasion.

Director: I persuaded them to see things clearly?

Friend: Yes.

Director: How did I do that?

3

Friend: How does persuasion typically work?

Director: You show them that there's a better way.

Friend: Then that's what you did. And they should be grateful for it. Or do you still think you receive as much benefit as you give?

Director: I still think that.

Friend: How does it help you if you help others get on a better way?

Director: I enjoy seeing people thrive.

Friend: That's it? It's that simple?

Director: Well, almost that simple.

Friend: What complicates things?

Director: It's not everyone that I like seeing thrive.

Friend: Who do you like to see thrive?

Director: People who deserve to thrive.

Friend: And these are the people you help?

Director: Yes.

Friend: What makes them worthy?

Director: It's hard to say.

Friend: Please try.

4

Director: They are concerned about the wellbeing of others.

Friend: You mean in the way that you are concerned with them?

Director: Yes.

Friend: Is the problem that they are concerned with everyone's wellbeing, while you are only concerned with the well being of those who are worthy?

Director: That's often a big part of the problem.

Friend: So you help them see with whom they ought to be concerned.

Director: Yes.

Friend: And then you hope that they will one day become like you, helping others who are worthy?

Director: In the best case, yes.

Friend: Do you think I am like this?

Director: I think you are worthy, Friend.

Friend: But do you think I help others who are worthy?

Director: Yes, but I've also seen you help some who are unworthy.

Friend: I know. I can't help it. I still feel that everyone deserves help.

Director: Well, Friend, either everyone deserves help or not everyone deserves help.

Friend: Maybe if I continue to observe who you help, I'll see who deserves help more clearly.

5

Director: From what you've seen so far in who I help, what have you learned?

Friend: Well.... I.... I'm not sure. What do you think I should have learned?

Director: I think you should have learned that there need not be any gratitude involved in the process.

Friend: But I can't help feeling that when you say that it's just a pose, that you really do hope for some gratitude. I know some people feel it after they've spoken with you.

Director: Well, they needn't.

Friend: Why deny them that feeling?

Director: Oh, I don't deny them it. I just don't think they need to feel it, that's all.

Friend: Is it a sign that they don't see things clearly?

Director: Yes. They can't see what I'm getting out of our exchange.

Friend: Do you think many people ever come to see this?

Director: Not many, no.

Friend: But maybe more than you think do.

Director: How so?

Friend: Maybe they see it's an even exchange and still feel gratitude for it.

Director: Why do you think someone should feel gratitude for an even exchange?

Friend: Not everyone is willing to make an even exchange. A true even exchange is, I think, something rather rare.

6

Director: You may be on to something, Friend.

Friend: Really? What?

Director: A true even exchange would allow for mutual gratitude, wouldn't it — gratitude going both ways, evenly?

Friend: Yes.

Director: Well, this must be what I was missing — the possibility of such an exchange and such gratitude.

Friend: Ha! I helped you see something clearly!

Director: And I am grateful.

Friend: I think what you don't want is for people to feel they owe you something.

Director: Yes, I think you're right. They don't owe me anything.

Friend: And you don't owe them anything. Or do you think you do?

Director: I must admit, I often feel I do.

Friend: But what could you possibly owe to someone you helped?

Director: Maybe my help wasn't good enough. Maybe I could have been more persuasive. Maybe I could have helped make things more clear.

Friend: Why do you think you owe all that to them?

Director: I feel it's my duty.

Friend: Your duty?

Director: Yes. To humanity.

7

Friend: What exactly are you trying to persuade people to see?

Director: Other people for what they are.

Friend: You mean the divide between the worthy and the unworthy?

Director: Yes. In the end, isn't that what counts?

Friend: I suppose that's true. But you know what the next question is?

Director: What?

Friend: Who are you to judge?

Director: But if not me — if not us — then who? Or do you think we don't need to judge?

Friend: No, I suppose we do.

Director: So I guess I am persuading people to judge, to learn to exercise their judgment. Is that so bad a thing?

Friend: No, not at all. It's a good thing, Director.

Director: And I don't want them to judge the way that I judge. I want them to judge on their own.

Friend: And their first judgment should be that they don't owe you anything.

Director: That's right.

Friend: But they can feel gratitude toward you, and you toward them.

Director: Indeed.

Friend: This sounds like a good way to go.

8

Director: Mutual gratitude can be the basis for friendship, no?

Friend: Definitely. You know, I feel gratitude toward you, Director, for helping me see things more clearly.

Director: And I feel gratitude to you, Friend, for seeing things more clearly, and for helping me to see things more clearly.

Friend: How does that really work for you, your feeling gratitude for my seeing things more clearly?

Director: It's rather simple. Learning to see better can be very difficult. I appreciate the effort you made.

Friend: Thanks.

Director: But there's more. As I watch you learning to see better, I learn, too.

Friend: But what do you learn?

Director: I gain a better understanding of the way things are.

Friend: Can you be more specific?

Director: When you learn to see something, you either confirm what I think I know or call it into question.

Friend: You mean you trust my eyes more than your own?

Director: Let's say they're a check on my own eyes. If you independently confirm what I think I see, great. If not, I might need to examine my view more closely.

Friend: So you really do get something out of helping people.

Director: Yes. I'm far from always being right, you know. That's why I try to persuade people to see with their own eyes rather than tell them what to see.

Friend: And you are grateful when they do. And they are grateful to you. Even.

Persons of the Dialogue

Director

Friend

1

Director: What is an impression?

Friend: It's something that is memorable about a person.

Director: Does everyone want to make an impression?

Friend: Well, everyone wants to make a good impression.

Director: Can you control what impression you make?

Friend: To a certain degree, I suppose.

Director: How do you do this?

Friend: You try to do all the right things.

Director: What if they're not right in the eyes of the person you're trying to impress?

Friend: Then you make a bad impression.

Director: So if you want to make a good impression you need to know your audience.

Friend: Yes.

Director: How do you do that?

Friend: I suppose you have to study your audience ahead of time.

Director: Is that easier to do when the audience consists of one or many?

Friend: One.

2

Director: How do you study someone?

Friend: I guess you have to ask around about him.

Director: So you get other people's impressions.

Friend: Yes.

Director: You learn what kind of impression he makes.

Friend: That's right.

Director: What if he makes different impressions on different people?

Friend: You have to learn what these people are like in order to understand why different impressions were made.

Director: How do you do this?

Friend: You talk to them. You spend time with them.

Director: And you can't do this with the one you wish to impress because in the process of getting to know him you would be making an impression.

Friend: Right.

Director: But maybe that's exactly the kind of impression you should make.

Friend: You mean, that I'm willing to get to know him?

Director: Yes. Wouldn't that be a good impression?

Friend: I suppose it would. But what happens when I get to know him?

Director: That's up to you.

3

Friend: What if he makes a bad impression on me?

Director: Then maybe you don't care what kind of impression you make on him.

Friend: But I set out to make a good impression on him.

Director: Sometimes in life we have to change course, Friend.

Friend: So are you saying I should never try to make a good impression on someone who makes a bad impression on me?

Director: Why would you want to?

Friend: Sometimes you need to.

Director: This doesn't sound like a good business to me.

Friend: People don't always have the luxury to make a bad impression, Director.

Director: But what are we talking about? Didn't we say that trying to get to know someone makes a good impression? Even if that person makes a bad impression on you, wouldn't you be making a good impression on him?

Friend: Not everyone wants you to know what they are truly like.

Director: Ah, I see. So you would be making a bad impression by trying to get to know him.

Friend: Exactly.

Director: Then who cares?

Friend: I do — if I need to make a good impression on him.

4

Director: You mean you'd be willing to live in ignorance of what he is like?

Friend: Yes, while I'm making my impression, at least.

Director: What need could you possibly have that would justify that?

Friend: Suppose I need a job from him.

Director: Are you saying you'd be willing to work for someone like that?

Friend: Sometimes you don't have a choice.

Director: Alright. Let's suppose you have no choice. What kind of impression do you need to make on him?

Friend: I need to show him that I'm not the type to question too much.

Director: You want him to think you're docile.

Friend: Yes.

Director: You know, Friend, when you pretend to be docile, you actually are docile. Are you really willing to be like that?

Friend: For the sake of argument, let's say I am.

Director: Alright. So you obtain employment with the man who doesn't want to be known. Do you get to know him now?

Friend: I get to see what he does, how he treats people.

Director: And I suppose this will all make a bad impression on you.

Friend: Yes.

5

Director: Do you think he will make this same bad impression on your new peers?

Friend: I don't see how he couldn't.

Director: What kind of impression will you make on your peers?

Friend: Well, I suppose they will take me to be docile.

Director: And they would be right.

Friend: True.

Director: Would you be happy to make that kind of impression?

Friend: No.

Director: So how can you possibly think you would be happy in this new role of yours?

Friend: Sometimes necessity trumps happiness, Director.

Director: There's always another way, Friend.

Friend: Is there? Is there really? Suppose this job is the only one I can get. What do I do?

Director: You think if you ask too many questions you won't get the job?

Friend: Yes.

Director: But you're going to take this job no matter what questions you ask or don't ask, right?

Friend: Right, if I'm offered it.

6

Director: Well, I think you should ask at least one pointed question, and do it in as nonchalant a manner as possible.

Friend: Why?

Director: You set the precedent. You won't quite make an impression as a trouble maker, but you will set the expectation that you will ask a tough question now and then.

Friend: This will help me with my impression on my peers. I can develop a reputation for the occasional tough question with them, too.

Director: What if your questions frighten those who are completely docile?

Friend: If they are frightened, then I suppose they might report me to the boss.

Director: So you don't want to frighten them?

Friend: No, I suppose I don't.

Director: So you reduce yourself to the lower common denominator, no?

Friend: I'm afraid that's how it would be.

Director: Do you want to live like that?

Friend: No.

Director: Then it's time to find another way.

Friend: Tell me what other way there is.

Director: Don't worry about the impression you make.

Friend: But how can I do that?

7

Director: Do you know, to a certainty, what sort of impression you'll make if you act a certain way?

Friend: Well, maybe not to a certainty — but to a great deal of likelihood.

Director: How can you know that?

Friend: I know how people are.

Director: That's your mistake. You can know how people generally are. But you don't know how a particular person is until you get to know him. And part of getting to know someone is making and receiving impressions. You don't know until you know, and by then it's too late to do anything about it. So tell me, Friend, would you rather be yourself or pretend to be someone else?

Friend: When you pretend you're someone else you actually are someone else, right?

Director: Right.

Friend: So I suppose I should be myself.

Director: Does any other way make sense?

Friend: No, it doesn't.

Director: What do you do when you come across someone who doesn't want to be known?

Friend: I decide that nothing good can come of a relationship with such a person.

Director: Even if this means not getting the job?

Friend: Even if it means not getting the job.

Director: I think you need to have faith.

Friend: Faith?

Director: Yes. Faith that someone will take you for what you really are, and appreciate you.

Friend: I'd like that.

Director: Then stick to your guns.

NATURAL

Persons of the Dialogue

Director

Friend

1

Friend: I want to be a natural at something.

Director: What do you mean by that?

Friend: I mean I want to be gifted at something.

Director: You mean you don't want to have to work too hard to be good at something?

Friend: Honestly? Yes.

Director: Would you settle to be a natural liar, or a natural braggart?

Friend: Oh, come on. You know what I mean.

Director: You want to be good at something good, something people respect.

Friend: Exactly.

Director: But why not work hard for it? Don't people respect hard work?

Friend: Well, I suppose if I'm a natural and I work hard, no one will be able to touch me. If I'm not a natural, hard work might not be enough.

Director: What do you think you might be good at?

Friend: I don't know.

Director: I think you are a good friend. In fact, I'd even say you're a natural at being a friend.

Friend: Thank you, Director.

2

Director: But why do you look so down? Don't you think that's enough?

Friend: I want to be more than that.

Director: What do you want to be?

Friend: I don't know. Something more.

Director: But being a friend is being something, very much something.

Friend: I want to be something that everyone recognizes.

Director: You want to be famous?

Friend: Yes.

Director: At what? Some game?

Friend: When you put it that way, it doesn't sound so good. But I'm not good at any game.

Director: For the sake of argument, let's say you are. Which would you rather be? A famous player or a good friend?

Friend: But why does there have to be a choice? Why not be both?

Director: Suppose you can be both. Would you rather be a natural at a game that is popular in our country, or a natural at a game that is popular in another country?

Friend: In our country, of course.

Director: Why? Because you want to be famous, but famous among people like you?

Friend: Yes.

3

Director: What if the other country has twice as many people? You could be twice as famous.

Friend: I would still rather be famous in our country.

Director: Among people like you.

Friend: Well, of course not everyone in our country is like me.

Director: But you'd prefer to be known by those like you?

Friend: I guess.

Director: And who is like you?

Friend: You are.

Director: What do we have in common?

Friend: Friendship.

Director: What else?

Friend: Philosophy.

Director: What else?

Friend: We share many tastes.

Director: Why not be famous among people like this, people with whom you fit naturally?

Friend: But that's not really being famous.

Director: Why not?

Friend: Well... it's just not.

4

Director: What if you were famous like this within a broad circle that includes people you haven't met?

Friend: What do you mean?

Director: What if word about you spreads far and wide, and those who, were they nearer, would likely be your friends, and would share in philosophy with you, and would share with you your tastes — what if they knew all about you? Wouldn't you be famous among these people?

Friend: I suppose.

Director: So be what you are. Be a natural. And be content with this sort of fame.

Friend: But how would word about me spread far and wide?

Director: Through your friends, naturally.

Friend: And what will they say? That they know someone who is a good friend?

Director: Yes.

Friend: That hardly seems enough.

Director: If you were going to a faraway land, and a good friend of yours told you that he has a friend, a true friend, there, is there a chance you'd look him up when you arrived?

Friend: I think there is a very good chance.

Director: Thus fame spreads.

Friend: But that's a very slow way to spread fame.

Director: You'd rather be famous indiscriminately?

Friend: What do you mean?

5

Director: Would you rather be famous among those who are unlike you and don't know you, or among those who are like you and know you?

Friend: Well, when you put it like that....

Director: Which sort of fame would be more significant, more meaningful?

Friend: The sort where everyone is like you and knows you, I suppose.

Director: Is this only possible in a relatively small community?

Friend: Yes.

Director: A community of peers?

Friend: That would be best.

Director: Natural peers?

Friend: Natural peers. True peers.

Director: Can you think of anyone by whom you'd rather be admired than your true, natural peers?

Friend: I can't. But how exactly are we peers?

Director: You treat one another as equals.

Friend: Even if we're really not equals?

Director: Let's just say you're more equal than not.

Friend: And that's good enough?

Director: I think it is.

6

Friend: Do you think I'm equal to you?

Director: Yes. You are my friend.

Friend: But if I weren't your friend?

Director: But you are.

Friend: Alright. Fair enough. So I'm a natural at being friends with certain types of people. But isn't everyone?

Director: Do you really think everyone has friends, true friends?

Friend: What do they have?

Director: Many have mere relationships of convenience, relationships that couldn't weather a storm.

Friend: But my friendships can?

Director: If you are the natural I think you are, then yes. Look, Friend. What's more important to you than friendship?

Friend: You mean, what's the most important thing to be a natural at? How about love?

Director: Ah, love. What does it mean to be a natural at love?

Friend: It means you are able to find it.

Director: But doesn't love happen when it will, despite our best efforts to find it? Isn't it out of our hands?

Friend: In a sense. But I believe you have to be prepared — emotionally mature, with strong life experience — in order to find true love, or for it to find you.

Director: That may be. But if you have to be prepared like that, can we say you are a natural?

7

Friend: That's an interesting point. Let's say you're not a natural at love if you have to be prepared. What do you think a natural in love is like?

Director: He is someone who — without being emotionally mature, without strong life experience — love strikes like a bolt of lightning, nearly killing him.

Friend: Ha! Your view of being a natural in love doesn't sound very good.

Director: It's not always good to be a natural.

Friend: Do you think all of us have to start out as naturals at love?

Director: Perhaps. But not all of us get struck by lightning.

Friend: What do you think accounts for the strikes?

Director: I'm inclined to ascribe it to luck.

Friend: Maybe the lightning is attracted to those who are more of a natural than others.

Director: That may be.

Friend: I think something similar happens with friendships.

Director: Please say more.

Friend: Friendships, as I see them, have, not lightening, but rather sparks, sparks that can't be controlled. You might find yourself a friend of someone you would never have expected to be friends with, simply because you felt a spark.

Director: Do you, a natural at friendship, see sparks of friendship where others see none?

Friend: Yes, I often do.

Director: Then that is your gift, Friend.

8

Friend: So you think I'd be a fool to waste my time and energy looking for something else to be a natural at, a fool to ignore the sparks that I already see.

Director: I think you should keep your eye on the sparks. And if you happen to see other sparks along the way, investigate them, too. Who knows what you'll come across on your way?

Friend: That's what I'll do. But tell me one thing, Director.

Director: Yes?

Friend: What are you a natural in?

Director: Philosophy.

Friend: How do you know?

Director: Because philosophy has its own sort of sparks, and I see them, Friend.

Friend: If these sparks are anything like the sparks of friendship I see, then, even though I enjoy philosophizing with you, I don't see them. So I guess I'm not a natural at philosophy.

Director: Are you okay with that?

Friend: As long as I have my own sparks of friendship, and manage not to get killed by a bolt of lightning, I am.

Director: Then you tend to your sparks, and I will tend to mine. And let's help each other with them whenever we can.

PERSISTENCE

Persons of the Dialogue

Director

Friend

1

Friend: I feel like giving up.

Director: But why?

Friend: I'm not getting anywhere with this.

Director: Where do you want to get to be?

Friend: I want to be good at it.

Director: You are good at it.

Friend: Thanks. But it seems like for every ten times I try only one comes out right.

Director: That sounds like a pretty good average for things like this.

Friend: You think so?

Director: Sure. You can't just keep on doing the same thing every time. You have to experiment. And if you're really experimenting, you're going to fail at times. In fact, the more bold you are in your experiments the more often you are likely to fail. But the end result is that your successful efforts are likely to be that much stronger than before, being infused with what you learned from your failures.

Friend: You make failure sound like not so bad a thing. But here's what I'm wondering now. Should I show people only my successes, or my failures, too?

Director: Do you know when something is a failure?

Friend: Sometimes I can tell. But most often not, until I have outside feedback.

Director: Then the only way to know you've failed is to show people everything, unless it's one of those times when you can tell.

2

Friend: But what if people, seeing so many failures, overlook the good, expecting that it, too, is a failure?

Director: Maybe what you need is a group of people who believe in you and aren't afraid to tell you when you've failed. They'll be on the lookout for something good from you, no matter how many failures they see. Then you can pass along what they affirm to your broader audience.

Friend: I like that idea. But I wonder. Won't that put a lot of pressure on the group that believes in me? After all, they are pronouncing whether something is a success or a failure.

Director: Would you rather go directly to your broader audience?

Friend: Maybe I have to.

Director: Isn't there anything that you can do before going to them?

Friend: Maybe there's a way for me to get good at knowing whether what I've done is a success or not.

Director: Why do you have problems in this regard?

Friend: Maybe it's because I'm too close to my work.

Director: You mean that you've put so much into it that you've lost perspective?

Friend: Yes, exactly. I think I need to be able to step back.

Director: Are there other reasons why you have problems knowing?

Friend: Maybe my taste is quirky. I mean, something might taste good to me that others will spit out as soon as they take a bite.

Director: Then you have to hope for others with quirky taste being in your broader audience.

3

Friend: But then I sometimes wonder. Is saying that you have quirky taste really just an excuse for not creating something that's very good? I mean, maybe I need to make something very good that has just a touch of quirkiness, as opposed to making something that isn't very good that is very quirky.

Director: That sounds like a good plan. Quirkiness is the spice, not the meat.

Friend: Yes, exactly.

Director: Can you tell the difference between the quirky and the good?

Friend: I know what they feel like. The inspiration for the quirky happens in a flash. Obtaining the good takes persistence.

Director: Why?

Friend: I don't know. That's just how it is.

Director: Which do you enjoy more, working on the meat or working on the spice?

Friend: I confess my weakness — I enjoy working on the spice most.

Director: Are you tempted to neglect the meat?

Friend: Yes, I'm somewhat ashamed to admit.

Director: Do you think this might be why you have so many failures?

Friend: Yes.

Director: So you know what to do then, don't you?

Friend: Yes, I have to focus on the meat and only add the spice as the finishing touch.

4

Director: But don't people often work the spice in before they start cooking?

Friend: Yes, that's true. So you're saying I should work it in from the outset?

Director: Yes. Have a plan, a plan that includes room for inspiration.

Friend: That means I work away until inspiration comes along, heed it, but then go back to persisting in my plan once it's gone?

Director: What do you think?

Friend: I think it's better than what happened in the past, when inspiration would knock me off of my plan and keep me from going back to it.

Director: Have you always had a plan going into things?

Friend: Often times, yes. But sometimes I have just relied on inspiration to show me the way.

Director: How did that work out?

Friend: Lots of spice, little to no meat. But what if I plan for inspiration and it doesn't come?

Director: Are you any worse off than if you didn't plan for it?

Friend: No, I guess not. I can always tighten up the plan.

Director: So now you know what to do as far as plans are concerned?

Friend: Yes.

Director: Now tell me, Friend. Would you rather have one brilliant work or ten mediocre works?

Friend: I'd rather have the one brilliant work. But if the question is between one brilliant work and ten very good works? I'd still choose the one brilliant work.

Director: Why?

5

Friend: Because I want to do the best work I possibly can, regardless if it means it doesn't happen very often. Ten very good works — nay, a hundred very good works — don't add up to one brilliant work. But the light from a brilliant work can shine down on even your mediocre works and lend them some sparkle.

Director: You mean the seeds of the brilliant may be seen in even the mediocre works of the one who achieved brilliance?

Friend: Yes, exactly.

Director: What does it take to achieve brilliance?

Friend: Very good work elevated by inspiration into brilliance.

Director: What does very good work require?

Friend: Patience. Persistence. Things I often sorely lack.

Director: And what do those things require?

Friend: Faith.

Director: Faith in what?

Friend: Yourself. Faith that you are capable and inspired.

Director: Why can't you just know that you are both capable and inspired? Is this some sort of false modesty on your part? I know you to be both capable and inspired.

Friend: Thank you, Director. But it's one thing to have been capable and inspired in the past, and quite another thing to be capable and inspired again.

Director: As far as capability goes, as long as you apply yourself diligently, I see no reason why there's any question of your being capable again. But as for being inspired, maybe there is a mystery here into which I have not been initiated.

Friend: Ha! You are one of the most inspired, and inspiring, people I know.

Director: Have I inspired you here today?

Friend: You have. I no longer feel like giving up. So thank you.

Director: What if it takes you a hundred mediocre works to achieve your one brilliant work?

Friend: I don't care if it takes a thousand. Well, I care. But you know what I mean. I'll try.

When

Persons of the Dialogue

Director

Friend

1

Friend: How do you know when enough is enough and it's time to give up?

Director: What are you thinking of giving up?

Friend: Writing.

Director: Oh? What are you writing?

Friend: A story. But it's not going very well.

Director: What's wrong with it?

Friend: The plot isn't working.

Director: Have you tried to fix it?

Friend: Many times.

Director: Why can't you?

Friend: I don't know what it should be.

Director: You mean you're writing but you don't know what you're writing about?

Friend: Exactly.

Director: Why are you writing?

Friend: I thought I had something to say. But now I'm not so sure.

Director: What did you want to say?

Friend: I wanted to — you're going to laugh — express myself.

2

Director: I don't see anything funny in that. But what did you want to express in particular?

Friend: The way I feel about things.

Director: How do you feel about things?

Friend: That's the problem. I'm not sure. Sometimes things seem one way to me. Sometimes they seem another way.

Director: Maybe you need to get straight on how you feel about things before you try to write.

Friend: How can I do that?

Director: Maybe talking about it will help.

Friend: Well, what I want to talk about is how you know when it's time to quit.

Director: Maybe it's time to quit when you can't talk about what you're doing anymore.

Friend: You think so? Why?

Director: What is writing but a sort of talking?

Friend: That's a good point.

Director: Which do you find easier, writing or talking?

Friend: Talking.

Director: What do you like to talk about?

Friend: I like to talk about philosophy, with you.

Director: Why don't you write about that?

3

Friend: Because I only talk about philosophy when I'm with you.

Director: You mean you can't think about it on your own?

Friend: I've tried, but I never seem to think of anything interesting along those lines — at least not as interesting as what you come up with. Will you help me?

Director: Yes, as long as you can at least come up with an interesting topic.

Friend: What if I can't?

Director: You'll have to think harder.

Friend: I think I have a topic.

Director: So soon? What is it?

Friend: Giving up. I'll write about that. I'll write, "It's time to quit when you can't talk about what you're doing anymore."

Director: What will you say, other than that?

Friend: That's where you come in.

Director: Oh no. I'm just lending a hand. You still have to do the work.

Friend: Well, I'll just have to sit at my computer and see what comes to me.

Director: You mean you can't talk about it now? Tell me, what do you think about the opposite possibility of what you're proposing to write?

Friend: Which is?

4

Director: When you can't talk about something, that is precisely when you shouldn't give up on it.

Friend: Why, because there's always something to say under the right circumstances, if only you can find them?

Director: Yes, that's a good way to look at it.

Friend: Yes, and maybe this thing you can't talk about is painful to bring up, but it needs to be brought up, one way or another, so it doesn't fester. If you give up on it you'll get sick.

Director: It seems you're getting the idea. Let's switch back. Why else might you not be able to talk about something, aside from it being time to quit?

Friend: Maybe you don't know anything about the subject.

Director: You mean you simply have nothing, nothing helpful or true, to say?

Friend: Yes. So maybe you should give up on things you know nothing about.

Director: Or maybe you should try to learn about them.

Friend: True, but when should you give up on learning?

Director: How about never?

Friend: But what if you're wasting your time trying to learn, as I am with trying to write my story?

Director: Maybe you're not wasting your time with your story.

Friend: But it feels like I am.

Director: Why, because it's difficult to write?

Friend: I wish it were difficult because that would mean I'm actually writing it.

Right now I'm not writing anything. I'm just obsessing over the plot.

5

Director: Can't you work something about giving up into what you've got now?

Friend: I'd like to, but how?

Director: How do you want the story to end? Try starting there. Do you want it to be a triumph that comes of never giving up? Or do you want it to be more ambiguous, where not giving up brings no clear victory?

Friend: Which do you think is more realistic?

Director: Both seem realistic to me.

Friend: Then maybe I'll include both.

Director: That sounds fine. What about someone who gives up? Are you going to have someone like that in there?

Friend: Yes, I think I should.

Director: Will the person who gives up come to a bad end? Or will giving up result in something new and wonderful happening to the character in question?

Friend: I don't know. What's an example of something new and wonderful happening?

Director: Oh, say someone is so bent on an ambition of his that he doesn't have time to stop and smell the roses. Make him stop and smell them. Something like that.

Friend: How will he be persuaded to quit?

Director: Maybe he doesn't even have to quit. Maybe he simply becomes less intense in his ambition. There are many possibilities, you know.

6

Friend: I'll have to decide how I feel about the various possibilities. And who knows? Maybe I'll include an example of each and let my audience decide which one they prefer. Let's suppose I go home and write these things up in the story. What if I bring it to you and you don't think it's very good? What would you say?

Director: I'd say that it's not very good.

Friend: When would you tell me to give up?

Director: If I were ever to tell you that, it would be when your expectations for success get the better of you.

Friend: You mean if I'm being hopelessly unrealistic.

Director: Yes.

Friend: Well, I just want to write for my friends. I don't expect that millions of people will read my writing.

Director: Then I don't think you should give up.

Friend: Even if what I'm writing isn't very good?

Director: What happens in the worst case? You give us something to discuss.

Friend: And I can learn from the discussions. Maybe my writing will improve.

Director: Exactly.

Friend: Well, I won't give up — though I'm going to need some encouragement here and there.

Director: You'll have it.

Friend: But what happens in the best case?

Director: You give us something wonderful — and you feel proud.

Friend: That would itself be wonderful.

Director: Would it be worth the effort, even if it's a great effort?

Friend: The only answer is yes.

Director: Then get to work.

DARE

Persons of the Dialogue

Director

Friend

1

Friend: I want to be more daring.

Director: Why? So your life will be more exciting?

Friend: No, not that.

Director: What will you dare?

Friend: To be different.

Director: Just different for different's sake?

Friend: No, I'll have meaningful difference.

Director: What will you do to be different?

Friend: I'll be different by being myself.

Director: But isn't everyone himself?

Friend: Yes and no. Certainly everyone is himself. But not everyone acts like himself.

Director: Why on earth not?

Friend: They don't dare.

Director: You mean they're afraid to act like themselves?

Friend: Yes.

Director: This seems very strange.

Friend: It may be strange, but nothing is more true.

2

Director: But doesn't it bother them not to act like themselves?

Friend: Yes, I'm sure it does — because it bothers them when someone else dares to act like himself.

Director: How do they react to someone like that, a daring one?

Friend: They often turn on him.

Director: But why?

Friend: They feel that he makes them look bad.

Director: Because he is daring and they are not.

Friend: Exactly.

Director: And you admire someone like this.

Friend: I do.

Director: So what do you think is the first step to acting like yourself?

Friend: I don't know. You just have to do it.

Director: But don't you think you have to know yourself first?

Friend: Yes, I suppose that's true.

Director: How do you know yourself?

Friend: You listen to your inner voice.

Director: And what does this voice tell you?

3

Friend: It tells you what you think.

Director: And what you think is what you are?

Friend: It's a big part of it, at least.

Director: Would you include convictions, beliefs, and so on as part of what you think?

Friend: Yes, and acting on those things is what is daring.

Director: What if someone is convinced that he should be like everyone else, that he should take his lead from them? If he acts on that conviction, is he daring?

Friend: No, of course not. I wouldn't even call that a conviction.

Director: Is having a conviction something that necessarily goes against the crowd?

Friend: Yes. Crowds, or especially mobs, never have convictions. I suppose they can have superstitions, prejudices, and so on, but not convictions.

Director: Never? Interesting. What is a conviction?

Friend: Something that takes courage to live up to.

Director: And courage and daring go hand in hand.

Friend: Of course.

Director: Now, are you telling me that you don't currently live up to your convictions to the degree you'd like, that you're not daring enough?

Friend: That's right.

Director: Do you know what your convictions are?

4

Friend: Yes, I know my convictions.

Director: What are they?

Friend: First is to be honest.

Director: Will you be honest to the conviction-less mob even as it turns on you for being an individual?

Friend: Well, I don't know. What do you think?

Director: What's the benefit of being honest to a mob?

Friend: You're true to yourself.

Director: Is the mob honest with you?

Friend: I don't know.

Director: Why not?

Friend: The mob doesn't like that I'm an individual, and it tells me so. Isn't that honesty?

Director: Maybe more than honesty is at stake here. What other convictions have you got?

Friend: I believe it is good to stand up for my friends.

Director: Against the mob.

Friend: If need be, yes.

Director: Have you done this?

Friend: Not as often I should have.

5

Director: And that's one of the reasons you're feeling less than daring.

Friend: Yes.

Director: Do you think you're different when you dare to stand up for your friends?

Friend: I do.

Director: Because most people don't stand up for their friends?

Friend: Well, not as many do as should, at least.

Director: What other convictions have you got besides honesty and sticking up for friends?

Friend: Those are the main ones.

Director: I see. Maybe there's another you should consider.

Friend: What?

Director: You want to be different, right?

Friend: Right.

Director: Now, you'll be different from a great many if you are completely honest and always stand up for your friends. But what if you also defy the mob by attacking its superstitions and prejudices, as a matter of conviction? That would take some daring, no?

Friend: It certainly would. But how would I go about this?

Director: It seems there are two ways. Address the mob as a whole, or address its component parts. Which do you think would work better?

Friend: The mob as a whole won't listen. So it's got to be the parts. But how would I go about this?

6

Director: Find a weak link and start there.

Friend: You mean someone who is not as enthusiastic about being part of the mob as the others?

Director: Yes.

Friend: And what do I say?

Director: Just pick one of the mob's prejudices to talk about, and be honest.

Friend: That's it?

Director: That's it. You'd be surprised what can come of simple talk like this.

Friend: The others in the mob won't appreciate this simple talk.

Director: You'll have to catch your man when he's alone.

Friend: And what happens if he reports our little chat back to the mob? Won't I become a target?

Director: You have to feel out how much you can safely say, Friend.

Friend: Yes, but what if this person is one way with me and another with the mob? What if he turns on me behind my back, and the mob comes after me for going against its prejudices?

Director: That's the risk.

Friend: So you're suggesting I have to pick my man carefully. Not only does he have to be a weak link, he has to be something else, doesn't he? What?

Director: He has to be a potential friend.

7

Friend: You mean he has to have some goodness in him. So if he talks honestly with me, and he shows signs of being willing to stick up for me as a friend, he's the one.

Director: He's the one who might break free of the mob.

Friend: Do you think it's harder to break free than it is never to have joined?

Director: I don't know, Friend. I never joined. But I suspect it's very difficult to break free. And I suspect relapses are likely.

Friend: Relapses? Why do I want as my friend someone who relapses? What if he turns the mob against me in one of these relapses?

Director: You're the one who said he wanted to be more daring.

Friend: Well, part of me wants to dare, but part of me says that I need to be more prudent.

Director: Then maybe you should do some preliminary daring before you think about taking on the mob.

Friend: That sounds good. What should I do?

Director: We said that being yourself largely amounts to what you think. And we included convictions under this heading. But there's more to thinking than having convictions. Dare to differ in what you think, Friend. Dare to differ in what you think.

Friend: You mean like not believing in the superstitions and prejudices of the mob?

Director: Yes, but there are more superstitions and prejudices in the world than those of the mob, or any simple crowd. Dare to think against them all. And then, if you want to take on a weak link, any weak link, you'll be all the better prepared. Dare what you can. Only you know what that is. And don't be too hard on yourself. We're all learners when it comes to things like this.

CONNECTING

Persons of the Dialogue

Director

Friend

1

Director: How did the interview go?

Friend: I don't know how to put it other than to say we didn't connect.

Director: What do you mean?

Friend: I mean when I spoke I felt like I was underwater and he couldn't hear me.

Director: I'm sorry to hear it, Friend. But why do you look so upset?

Friend: I really wanted this job.

Director: Maybe you'll get it. Maybe he felt differently.

Friend: I don't want a job where I feel like I can't connect with my boss.

Director: Maybe he'd be different once you get to work.

Friend: I doubt it. My gut tells me there's simply no connection there.

Director: So will you turn down the job if you are offered it?

Friend: How can I do that? I don't have any other prospects.

Director: Were you yourself on the interview, or were you acting?

Friend: I was myself.

Director: What's wrong with a company that hires you for being yourself?

Friend: Well, when you put it like that it doesn't sound so bad.

2

Director: Maybe you can keep your time interacting with this boss of yours to a minimum.

Friend: Yes, I think I have to.

Director: Did he seem like a micromanager to you?

Friend: No, not particularly.

Director: That's good, isn't it?

Friend: I suppose. Do you connect with your boss?

Director: Yes, I do.

Friend: He really listens to you?

Director: Yes.

Friend: And he doesn't micromanage you?

Director: No, he doesn't.

Friend: You're lucky.

Director: Maybe there's a way you can get your boss to listen.

Friend: How?

Director: Show him that he needs you. Become invaluable to him.

Friend: How do I do that?

Director: Be as competent at your job as you can.

3

Friend: What if we still don't connect?

Director: Then he has problems of his own that he should be concerned about. A manager should always connect with his reports, and especially with those who do their jobs very well. If he's not doing this, there will be others who notice.

Friend: What if there aren't?

Director: Then you're not in a good place and should be looking for another job. What if you try to find out in advance if there are other people who would and do notice, people you can connect with?

Friend: How?

Director: Ask to meet with more people. See if you connect with them.

Friend: That's a good idea. But it won't change the fact that I don't connect with my boss.

Director: True, but it's better to have some amount of connection than none, wouldn't you agree?

Friend: That's true. I'll see if I can meet with more people. But let's say I connect with my boss's peers, and even his boss. Do I hint that there's something wrong with my boss?

Director: I would follow their lead and be careful. No one likes a disloyal employee. If you're disloyal to your boss, how will you be to a new boss?

Friend: If the new boss deserves loyalty I would be loyal.

Director: Yes, but how is the new boss to know what you consider worthy of loyalty? What if he has to make a difficult decision? Is he left wondering whether you'll abandon him and talk about him to others?

Friend: Then how am I going to get word out about my boss?

4

Director: People have eyes, Friend. They know what he's like. But he's there for a reason. Maybe you can find out what that reason is.

Friend: Oh great. The boss I don't connect with is there for a reason. Maybe I can find a better reason, one that makes him leave the company.

Director: Are you suggesting that you would be that reason, that you would take over your boss's job?

Friend: Maybe I could, in time.

Director: But if you're a good employee, you'll make your boss look good, right?

Friend: I suppose. But are you now suggesting I should be less than a good employee?

Director: That's the dilemma, Friend. If you're good, you make your boss look good. If you're less than good, you do make your boss look less than good, but you look less than good, too, so you wouldn't be a good candidate to take over his job.

Friend: I'm doomed either way in a situation like this. Maybe I shouldn't take the job.

Director: Maybe there's another way. You want to do your boss in, right? I mean, he doesn't connect with you.

Friend: Yes, I want to do him in.

Director: But you want to do him in without doing yourself in, right?

Friend: That's right.

Director: What if you make his peers and his boss look good?

Friend: What do you mean?

5

Director: Take on extra work for these people. Do a great job. Make them look good. But keep what you do for them a secret. You don't want any credit for this work.

Friend: But I'm still making my boss look good?

Director: No. Skimp on your work for him while doing all of this extra work for others. Do enough to get by, of course. But don't shine for him. And don't let him know what you're doing for others.

Friend: Do great work for others, but only okay work for him. And be a sneak.

Director: Exactly.

Friend: I can't tell if you're kidding. Won't my boss get mad?

Director: He very well may. Can you live with that?

Friend: If he's completely unconnected with me, yes.

Director: Why do you think he's unconnected?

Friend: Because he's arrogant. That's the sense I got when I met with him.

Director: And arrogance deserves punishment.

Friend: It does.

Director: And you'll punish him by holding back, by being just okay in what you do for him.

Friend: Yes. This idea is growing on me.

Director: Do you expect that the others you help — his peers, his boss — will be loyal to you?

Friend: Why wouldn't they be?

6

Director: Not everyone is as naturally loyal as you are, Friend. You need to find ways to make them loyal.

Friend: How do I do that?

Director: You make them need you.

Friend: How?

Director: Take on essential work for them, things they can't do without, things they cannot do themselves.

Friend: And hold them hostage?

Director: Can you stomach it?

Friend: But this is so Machiavellian.

Director: Do you think the modern day workplace is anything less than that?

Friend: I guess I've been naive. So I hold them hostage. What then?

Director: Imply to these people that you might leave off what you are doing for them in order to focus on making your boss look good.

Friend: They'll turn on my boss, won't they?

Director: If all goes well.

Friend: I'm starting to feel sorry for him.

Director: Why?

Friend: No one wants to have everyone turn against you.

Director: And no one wants to work for a boss he can't connect with.

7

Friend: What about my peers?

Director: What about them?

Friend: Do I keep them in the dark?

Director: What would you have them know? That you are trying to undermine your boss?

Friend: Wouldn't it help to have allies in this effort?

Director: So you can have competitors for your boss's job when he's finally removed?

Friend: That's a good point. This is a lonely business, isn't it?

Director: None lonelier. It's not for everyone, Friend. And I wouldn't say it's "good."

Friend: Have you ever done something like this, Director?

Director: Me? I don't want anyone else's job. And I never have. You have to decide what you want.

Friend: Maybe I should just live with not connecting with my boss. And who knows? I might not even get the job.

OPEN-MINDED

Persons of the Dialogue

Director

Friend

1

Director: Friend, what does it mean to be open-minded?

Friend: Why are you asking me?

Director: Because someone recently told me that you are not very open-minded.

Friend: Who?

Director: I'd rather not say. So, do you think you are open-minded?

Friend: It depends. I'm open with my friends, but not with others. Does that make me closed-minded?

Director: It's yet to be seen. What does it mean to be open-minded?

Friend: It means to be receptive to arguments and ideas.

Director: Are you?

Friend: No, of course not. Arguments and ideas are bad news for the most part.

Director: Why is that?

Friend: Most arguments are meant to win you over to the side of the person making the argument — and that usually involves having you do something in his interest. It's the same with ideas.

Director: These things are all about interest?

Friend: Of course they are.

Director: What about when an argument or an idea is coming from a friend?

Friend: I don't mind serving the interest of my friends.

2

Director: But don't you think an argument or an idea can amount to more than that, mere interest?

Friend: No, not really. Give me an example of an argument or an idea that's not ultimately rooted in someone's interest.

Director: How about the idea of selflessness?

Friend: Ha! That one especially is rooted in the interest of the person who is presenting it.

Director: And all arguments and ideas along these lines are hypocritical?

Friend: All of them. Don't you agree?

Director: I'm not sure I do. Do your friends make arguments like these, selfless ones?

Friend: No, they know better. They're much more straight forward. And they're not hypocritical.

Director: But what if you found someone who wasn't hypocritical, who was making selfless sorts of arguments?

Friend: You mean what if I encountered a person wrapped up in fantasy?

Director: You wouldn't be open-minded?

Friend: No, I would just laugh. Are you open-minded, Director?

Director: Yes, I am.

Friend: Even to hypocrites and fantasists?

Director: I'm open to many arguments and ideas.

Friend: But why?

3

Director: Because if I come across hypocrites and fantasists, or anyone else along these lines, I try to listen, and then sometimes I engage with them and try to show them that their arguments and ideas are no good.

Friend: Why do you waste your time like that?

Director: I don't consider it a waste of time.

Friend: But what if they're not persuaded?

Director: At least I've had my say. And who knows? Others who were listening in may have been persuaded.

Friend: Do any of the arguments and ideas you expose yourself to actually benefit you?

Director: Oh, yes — sometimes.

Friend: How do they benefit you? Do you come to believe them?

Director: No, generally speaking. But I learn something from them, if I can.

Friend: What?

Director: A new perspective.

Friend: And what good is this new perspective?

Director: It helps me understand the way others are. Don't you want to understand others, Friend?

Friend: Generally speaking, no — I don't.

Director: Maybe that's the difference between you and me. I want to understand. You don't.

4

Friend: I understand enough — what I need to understand.

Director: You and your friends share an understanding, right?

Friend: That's right.

Director: But what if you and your friends are wrong about some things? Won't your shared understanding land you in trouble?

Friend: So what do you suggest we do?

Director: Strive always to understand more.

Friend: Even from fools and manipulators?

Director: Even so. Try to understand all you can from all you encounter. That way you don't run the risk of the closed sect.

Friend: Which is?

Director: Disaster.

Friend: From being closed-minded?

Director: Exactly.

Friend: I don't know, Director. I'd rather risk it with my friends than deal with hypocrites and fools.

Director: And I, Friend, would rather risk it with both friends and those who seem at first to be hypocrites and fools. Maybe I can help you and your friends.

Friend: How?

5

Director: I can tell you about arguments and ideas I've come across that might prove beneficial to understand.

Friend: Well, I suppose understanding them wouldn't hurt. But what's in it for you?

Director: Me? I get to spread understanding. That's enough for me.

Friend: You're sounding awfully selfless, Director. That makes me nervous.

Director: Oh, don't be nervous. The spread of understanding is in my interest, Friend. The more that others understand what I understand, the happier I am. It's that simple.

Friend: I guess there's no harm in understanding. What's one of the things you've come across that you think I should understand?

Director: How some of the sincerely selfless can be brought around to know their own interests and to serve them, while maintaining the better parts of the virtue of selflessness. Isn't that something you'd like to understand?

Friend: But why, so I can help the selfless to stop floundering in selflessness? You assume I want to help others, when I'm really just content to help my friends.

Director: How do you choose your friends?

Friend: We have mutual interests.

Director: What if one of these selfless ones, who now helps himself, has mutual interests with you? Would you make him your friend? After all, through his habit of selflessness he's used to helping others. I'm sure he would help you if you became friends.

Friend: If he really had mutual interests with me, I would make him my friend.

Director: So you're open-minded about this.

Friend: Yes, I guess I am.

6

Director: I wonder what else you're open-minded about.

Friend: Director, I am open-minded about anything that it is in my interest.

Director: So you mustn't conceive of your interests too narrowly, as so many do.

Friend: What do you mean?

Director: Suppose you think it's not in your interest to know about a certain philosophy, and so you ignore someone who could teach you about it. What if it turns out that knowledge of this philosophy could result in your gaining many new friends?

Friend: I see your point. But I don't believe it's in someone's interest to have too many friends. A small group of good friends is best.

Director: Even if you could have a large group of good friends?

Friend: Yes, even so.

Director: Why?

Friend: You can be closer, more closely knit, with a small group of friends.

Director: What about acquaintances? Would you have a large circle of them?

Friend: Yes, I suppose.

Director: Well, suppose that knowing the philosophy we were speaking of could result in a large number of new acquaintances. Wouldn't that be to your benefit?

Friend: It would depend on the quality of the acquaintances.

Director: Suppose that the philosophy in question encourages virtue.

Friend: What sort of virtue?

Director: Honesty.

7

Friend: It would be good to have a large number of acquaintances who are honest. But I think your example is a bit too contrived. Honest men are not found in great numbers.

Director: But what if, among them all, you find one truly honest man? Would getting to know him be worth learning the philosophy?

Friend: Yes, I suppose it would.

Director: And so it may be with many other things, if only you are open to them.

Friend: But there are so many things one might be open to. You have to draw the line somewhere so you don't get overwhelmed. Where?

Director: You have to know how much you can take on, what your own capacity is. And then, after a while, you might develop a knack for what is likely to produce good results.

Friend: Will you help me until I develop my knack?

Director: Certainly.

Friend: Because you want to spread understanding, or because of something else?

Director: Because I want to spread understanding — and because I want to help my friend.

Exclamation Point

Persons of the Dialogue

Director

Customer

1

Customer: Director, I'm glad you're here. Look at this. I hate when people use "happy" exclamation points in their emails.

Director: Because you think it's phony excitement?

Customer: Yes, exactly. And even if the excitement is genuine, it's not manly to get that excited about things — and it suggests an inefficient frame of mind, too.

Director: You like an even tempered email.

Customer: I do.

Director: Do you ever use exclamation points?

Customer: Very, very rarely.

Director: Do you ever get excited?

Customer: Yes, of course I do. But I keep myself in check. I expect that others will do the same. Your emails are a good example. They're solid.

Director: But I have a confession to make. I use exclamation points in emails to others, to those who use exclamation points in turn.

Customer: You say different things to different people?

Director: I say the same things, but I say them differently. For instance, I might write to you: "I got the job." I might write to another: "I got the job!"

187

Customer: I suppose the latter would be appropriate if you were talking to children, and the like.

Director: How do you act around children? Do you put exclamation points at the end of what you say? Or are you manly and serious with them, too?

2

Customer: The time to be serious comes quickly enough. I talk to them with exclamation points — happy exclamation points, not the kind that come from anger. I love children.

Director: Can you love the child in the man?

Customer: Ha. You're very funny, Director. If we're talking about a business associate of mine, acting all excited like a child, I have no time for that at all. It tells me his mind isn't properly on his work. And it makes me question his judgment.

Director: Because he's not serious enough.

Customer: Right.

Director: Do you ever joke at work?

Customer: There are times when jokes are appropriate.

Director: But I take it that those times are few and far between.

Customer: The more serious I am at work, the better I perform. And the better I perform, the better I provide for my family. That doesn't leave much time for jokes.

Director: Will you tell me a joke?

Customer: I don't really have one to tell you.

Director: When's the last time you told a joke at work?

Customer: I guess.... Well, I guess I never have. But telling jokes and joking around are different things.

Director: When's the last time you joked around?

Customer: A couple of months ago one of the admins made a comical mistake. I joked about that. There, see? I, too, can appreciate humor.

3

Director: Good, then you'll appreciate the humor of this. I dare you to put a friendly exclamation point in your emails.

Customer: Dare me? Ha, ha. And what will I get for my effort?

Director: I think your workers will appreciate it.

Customer: Yes, but most of them are already exclaiming away. It's a problem.

We're not as efficient as we could be because of all this foolishness. Why should I encourage them?

Director: You see yourself as preventing the slide down the slippery slope into an anarchy of exclamation points, don't you? Each time an exclamation laden email arrives in your inbox you take delight on damping down on the tone in your reply, right?

Customer: But what's wrong with that? Someone has to hold the line. Nobody else in my office seems willing.

Director: You're a senior vice president. You have influence by virtue of your position. Do you think anyone would listen to you less if you started exclaiming in your emails?

Customer: Do you have any idea how hard I had to work to get to the point I'm at now? Do you have any idea how serious the people were who I reported to during my climb?

Director: They didn't use exclamation points?

Customer: Did they? Ha! They never used them. Ever. I remember when the company went public and everyone at the top made a great deal of money. Do you know what my boss wrote in a memo to his staff? "Things have turned out nicely." That was as excited as he got!

Director: Do you think he was more excited in person?

Customer: I was in his office when he wrote the memo. He was as buttoned up about the whole thing in person as he was in the memo.

4

Director: Maybe there was subtle humor there that you weren't picking up on. You were younger and less experienced then, right?

Customer: True. But I use subtle humor in my messages now.

Director: Who picks up on it?

Customer: I'm sure you would. And I think my admin does, at times.

Director: What do you think his messages are like?

Customer: Dry, like mine.

Director: I think his are a bit wry, too.

Customer: Oh, and mine aren't?

Director: Wryness is more appropriate for a subordinate, don't you think?

Customer: What do you think is appropriate for me?

Director: A dash of exclamation points here and there, Customer. Mix things up.

People will be pleasantly surprised, and you'll like the results.

Customer: What, you just want me to turn on a dime, change my ways out of nowhere?

Director: This is a winner for you, Customer. You'll be more popular.

Customer: I don't know. I'm not a populist. I'm wary of that.

Director: And you're going to hold off the dangers of populism by holding off on the exclamation points?

5

Customer: When I started working people wrote to each other with Dear Sir and Yours Truly. It took me many years before I got to the point where I could drop those openings and closings.

Director: Why did you drop them?

Customer: Because I was the only one using them anymore, and, frankly, I started to feel foolish.

Director: Do you think you're the only one not using exclamation points?

Customer: If not the only one, then pretty darned close to it. But I don't feel foolish. I think those who use all those silly exclamation points are the fools.

Director: Do you think they are hypocrites, too?

Customer: You put your finger exactly on it. Some of my peers want to make it seem like it's all fun and games when, in fact, it's not at all fun and games — it's business. I'm honest when it comes to this. People respect that.

Director: Maybe you can continue to be honest but spice things up a bit — just a bit. Write five paragraphs that are serious and then close with a sixth that is punctuated with a friendly exclamation point, just one.

Customer: And that would be enough to get me to stop being a dinosaur?

Director: Yes, I believe it would.

Customer: Well, maybe I'll give it a try. Would you be willing to help me draft it?

Director: I can be in your office on Monday at ten. Want to do it then?

6

Customer: Yes. And thank you. But what if people respond to me with a gush of exclamation points?

Director: Stick to one exclamation point per message. They'll love it.

Customer: And it won't make me seem to be an excitable old fool to do this?

Director: Hardly. Don't worry. We'll draft your message with the greatest seriousness. In fact, it can be our little secret — you won't feel as light hearted as your message will imply. But that may change.

Customer: And that's exactly what I'm afraid of!

Director: Why, don't you want to be a bit more light hearted?

Customer: It might take my mind off of what's important.

Director: The state of your heart isn't important? I would say it's most important.

Customer: Look, I'm willing to try. But promise me you'll lend a hand even after the first message goes out?

Director: You have my word. We'll tame these monstrous exclamation points, you and I. And you can keep to your curmudgeonly ways when you write to me. Another little secret that we'll keep.